THE FIRST PRINCE OF WALES?

THE FIRST PRINCE OF WALES?

Bleddyn ap Cynfyn, 1063–75

Sean Davies

UNIVERSITY OF WALES PRESS
2016

www.uwp.co.uk

British Library Cataloguing-in-Publication Data
A catalogue record for this book is available from the British Library.

ISBN   978-1-78316-936-8
e-ISBN 978-1-78316-937-5

Typeset in Wales by Eira Fenn Gaunt, Cardiff
Printed by CPI Antony Rowe, Melksham

Contents

Acknowledgements

My first debt of gratitude goes to all the staff at the University of Wales Press. Finding support for any sort of research and writing on medieval Wales is obviously a huge challenge, and the Press's willingness and ability to get behind this sort of project helps to keep alive this neglected period of the country's history. The Press's care and attention to detail in the production process has been greatly appreciated. I also owe a huge thanks to Professor Huw Pryce of Bangor University; his response to an unheralded email requesting help with the section on Bleddyn's influence on Welsh law went above and beyond any expectation. Professor Pryce's detailed feedback deepened and transformed my own understanding of this area, although – of course – any mistakes remain mine. Finally, this work would not have been possible without the love and support of my mother, Monica, of my brother, Mike, his wife, Marie, and their son, Llywelyn; they will understand that this book is dedicated to my father, David James Davies, who we lost in 2014 but who lives with us every day.

List of Illustrations

List of Abbreviations

AC	*Annales Cambriae*, ed. J. Williams ab Ithel (London, 1860)
ANS	*Anglo Norman Studies*
Arch. Camb.	*Archaeologia Cambrensis*
ASC	*The Anglo-Saxon Chronicle*, ed. and trans. D. Whitelock (London, 1961). All given dates follow this edition
BBCS	*Bulletin of the Board of Celtic Studies*
Bren.	*Brenhinedd y Saeson or The Kings of the Saxons*, ed. and trans. T. Jones (Cardiff, 1971). All year references are to the amended dates given by Jones
Brut (Pen. 20)	*Brut y Tywysogyon or The Chronicle of the Princes, Peniarth MS. 20 Version*, ed. and trans. T. Jones (Cardiff, 1952). All year references are to the amended dates given by Jones
Brut (RBH)	*Brut y Tywysogyon or The Chronicle of the Princes, Red Book of Hergest Version*, ed. and trans. T. Jones (Cardiff, 1955). All year references are to the amended dates given by Jones

EHR	*English History Review*
Gruffudd ap Cynan	*Vita Griffini Filii Conani: The Medieval Life of Gruffudd ap Cynan*, ed. and trans. P. Russell (Cardiff, 2005)
Life of King Edward	*The Life of King Edward (who rests at Westminster, attributed to a monk of Saint Bertin)*, ed. and trans. F. Barlow (2nd edn, Oxford, 1992)
Map	Walter Map, *De Nugis Curialium / Courtiers' Trifles*, ed. and trans. M. R. James, C. N. L. Brooke and R. A. B. Mynors (Oxford, 1983)
NLWJ	National Library of Wales Journal
OV	Orderic Vitalis, *Historia Ecclesiastica*, ed. and trans. M. Chibnall, 6 vols (Oxford, 1969–80)
PBA	Proceedings of the British Academy
TCHS	*Transactions of the Caernarfonshire Historical Society*
THSC	*Transactions of the Honourable Society of Cymmrodorion*
TRHS	*Transactions of the Royal Historical Society*
TWNFC	*Transactions of the Woolhope Naturalists Field Club*
Vita	A. W. Wade-Evans (ed. and trans.), *Vitae Sanctorum Britanniae et Genealogiae* (Cardiff, 1944)
WHR	*Welsh History Review*

Introduction

Bleddyn ap Cynfyn's place in Welsh history is a somewhat curious one. Despite being one of the mightiest and most influential of native rulers his own deeds are largely unknown and he is mostly remembered for his place in the genealogies as the founder of the second dynasty of Powys. But to consider Bleddyn as a regional ruler restricted to a specific portion of mid Wales is to do a great disservice to his story and legacy. Bleddyn was a leader at the heart of the tumultuous events that forged Britain in the cauldron of Norman aggression in the mid-eleventh century. Having succeeded his half-brother Gruffudd ap Llywelyn in 1063, he always strived to reconstruct the fledgling kingdom of Wales that had been created by that remarkable ruler. To attempt to achieve this aim, Bleddyn built and maintained a key alliance with the Anglo-Saxon earls Edwin and Morcar, first against the Godwines and then in the bitter war of attrition against William the Conqueror and the Normans.

Such exploits on a grand scale were the backdrop to Bleddyn's ambitious plans for a kingdom of Wales. Secure in his heartlands of Gwynedd and Powys, he sought to impose his power on the rest of the country. While military might and strategic alliances were always central to such plans, Bleddyn was much more than a warlord. He is one of the few men acknowledged as a reformer of the laws of Hywel Dda and he was remembered in a version of the Welsh chronicle as 'a defender of orphans, the weak and widows, the strength of the learned and the churches, the comfort of the lands, generous towards all, terrible in war and lovable in peace, a defence for all'.

Despite such qualities, Bleddyn's reign was hamstrung by the problems that would bedevil Welsh rulers in the twelfth and thirteenth century; the competing ambitions of their own countrymen and the need for a strong ally across the English border. For all his wide-ranging ambitions, the nature of his rise to power and the events of his reign effectively ended the possibility of Wales ever becoming an independent, united realm under one native leader again. Instead, the groundwork was laid for the familiar, fragmented and bewildering network of petty Welsh 'kingdoms' and marcher lordships that characterised the country in the twelfth and thirteenth centuries. His reign began the age of the princes, which means that – in fact if not in title – he can be regarded as the first prince of Wales.

A note on dating

At the outset of this book it is important to acknowledge a problem with regard to the start date given in the title, 1063; the issue is that we cannot say with certainty whether or not the date – which signifies the start of the reign of Bleddyn and the death of his predecessor, Gruffudd ap Llywelyn – should in fact be 1064. The confusion is linked to the unknown date of the death of Earl Ælfgar of Mercia and to Harold Godwinesson's subsequent Christmas attack on Gruffudd in Rhuddlan. These events were traditionally thought to have occurred in late 1062, but Benjamin Hudson has put forward a strong case suggesting that they happened in late 1063.[1] If his argument is accepted, it would mean that Gruffudd's death – and the start of Bleddyn's reign – should be dated to 1064, not 1063.

The chronology involved in a study of the relevant source material – Welsh, English, Irish and Norman – is tortuous and contradictory; deciding to favour one source means choosing to disregard another. The various Welsh annals and the Anglo-Saxon Chronicle have 1063 as the year of Gruffudd's death, although the *Annales Cambriae* chronology is very confused for this period. Contemporary Irish chronicles and John of Worcester date Gruffudd's death to 1064 and, as Hudson notes, their precise chronological references to the Paschal cycle seem to offer more authority. One version of the later *Brutiau* explicitly refers to the Paschal cycle as giving the date as 1063; but this is in the unreliable *Bren.* text and it may have been an attempt by the author to 'correct' contradictory sources he had in front of him. Hudson's 1064 date for Gruffudd's death has recently found favour with Thomas Charles-Edwards in his magisterial *Wales and the Britons 350–1064*, but the vast majority of English and Welsh historians have favoured the traditional 1063 date; that list of historians includes Rees Davies, whose *The Age of Conquest: Wales, 1063–1415* comes from the same Oxford University Press *History of Wales* series as the Charles-Edwards book (although it was written before the Hudson article).

There does not seem to be a way to settle this debate definitively, but I favour 1063, which would fit with the generally accepted date of Ælfgar's death in 1062. It also fits more convincingly with other known chronology, notably the career of Harold. If we accept that Harold made a trip to Normandy in this period (some suggest that this was just Norman propaganda) it would most probably have been in 1064, a date that would mean his Welsh campaign must have been in 1062–3. The alternative date for the Norman excursion is early 1065, but this would have given Harold little opportunity to get back to England and order the building work at Portskewett that would play a prominent part in the events of that year. Harold's biographer Ian Walker contends that: 'Within this period, a visit to Normandy by Harold is probably best placed in 1064, since by then Maine had been conquered. William's expedition against Brittany, on which Harold is said to have accompanied him, probably also occurred in that year.'[2]

Although the uncertainty about the date of Gruffudd's death and the start of Bleddyn's reign is frustrating, it would seem to have little bearing on the arguments that follow, as we know nothing of events in Wales between the king's death and the 1065 building work at Portskewett. For the sake of readability, I have chosen to refer consistently to 1063 throughout the text of this book, rather than using 1063–4.

Notes

[1] See B. T. Hudson, 'The destruction of Gruffudd ap Llywelyn', *WHR* 15 (1991), 331–50; for further discussion, see K. L. Maund, 'Cynan ab Iago and the killing of Gruffudd ap Llywelyn', *CMCS* 10 (1985), 57–65.

[2] I. Walker, *The Last Anglo-Saxon King* (Stroud, 1997), p. 104.

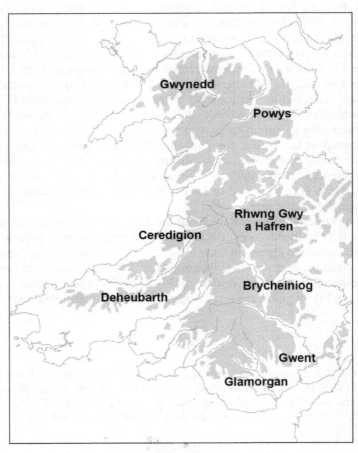

Figure 1 Kingdoms of medieval Wales

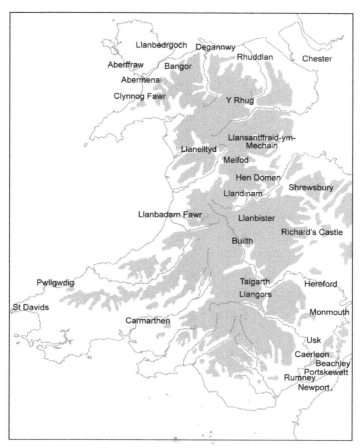

Figure 2 Key locations mentioned in the text

1

The Kingdoms Unite

One of the major reasons for the lack of acknowledgement that has been given to Bleddyn's true place in history is the version of Welsh history that was promoted by the princes of Gwynedd in the twelfth and thirteenth centuries. The resurgence of the dynasty of these princes can be attributed to the influential late-eleventh and early twelfth-century ruler Gruffudd ap Cynan. He was born an exile in Dublin, the son of a Welsh noble from a dynastic branch that had once enjoyed rule, but that was dangerously close to obscurity and extinction. The heartland of power for Gruffudd's forebears was Gwynedd, and when he and his descendants returned to prominence in the twelfth century they would use Gwynedd as the base to try to extend their dominion across native Wales. This has led many to suggest that Welsh kings such as Bleddyn, who ruled in the intervening period, were usurpers, regarded as somehow illegitimate.[1] There is little evidence of this in contemporary sources. Gruffudd ap Cynan's dynastic line had not enjoyed any sort of rule in Wales since 1039, and the earliest possible date at which Gruffudd could be considered to have a serious claim to Welsh kingship is 1081 (a date closer to 1100 is probably more realistic). The most significant rulers of north Wales in the intervening period were related quite closely to each other, but only distantly to Grufffudd's dynastic line. They also wielded far more power than Gruffudd ever did, and there is no suggestion in contemporary sources that they were regarded as anything other than legitimate rulers.

Whilst Bleddyn may be regarded as an usurping ruler if we accept the historical tradition that emerged from twelfth- and thirteenth-century Gwynedd, he is treated with respect in other traditions as he was the founder of the second dynasty of Powys. He is prominent in Welsh genealogies and to be able to trace descent to him was regarded as a great boon. The key to interpreting the disconnect between these two traditions and to understanding the true position of Bleddyn in the mid-eleventh century is to consider what had happened to Gwynedd and Powys in the centuries before his rule, and the years immediately following his demise.

The Merfyn Frych dynasty of Gwynedd

Gwynedd and Powys had, in fact, ceased to be separate kingdoms in the ninth century when the first dynasty of Powys had come to an end. After 854 there are no source references to Powys until the later eleventh century; Thomas Charles-Edwards says that the former king-dom was 'probably subsumed into Gwynedd for much of that period' and that it must be must be doubted whether anyone in eleventh- and twelfth-century Powys knew exactly what ninth-century Powys was composed of.[2] Evidence from the Pillar of Eliseg – a stone cross out-side Llangollen with inscriptions celebrating the first dynasty of Powys – suggests that the kings of the region had enjoyed a resurgence of power in the early to mid ninth century, when threats from the leaders of Mercia on their eastern borders had diminished. However, they soon faced a fresh challenge from the west. A vigorous new dynasty, that of Merfyn Frych, had come to power in Gwynedd, quite probably with Hiberno-Scandinavian support from the Irish Sea region. The last known king of the first dynasty of Powys, Cyngen ap Cadell, died in Rome in 854 and Charles-Edwards places the date of the final subjection of Powys to Gwynedd in the period 881–6.[3] After 854, the next mention of Powys in the Welsh chronicle comes in 1069 and even then it is only mentioned in one version (*Brut RBH*), where the region is treated as an appendage of Gwynedd. It is not until 1102 that all versions of the Welsh chronicle name Powys as an independent entity, separate from Gwynedd.[4] Gwynedd and Powys had effectively become a single kingdom of north Wales in the later ninth century, the development being part of a trend seen throughout Wales – and, indeed, throughout post-Roman western Europe – for small kingdoms to coalesce into larger ones. In other parts of post-Roman western Europe, some of these entities would later form nation states.

Llywelyn ap Seisyll and the resurgence of Powys

For most of the period in which Powys and Gwynedd were united, the latter was the dominant partner. The most likely scenario would seem to be that the Merfyn Frych dynasty of Gwynedd had forced its power on Powys in the ninth century, although in order to rule they would have had to rely on powerful local families which would seek to strengthen their own position. One such family was probably that of Llywelyn ap Seisyll, the head of a dynasty that would burst into the historical light in the early eleventh century, at the same time as we see a power shift from Gwynedd to Powys. The forebears of Llywelyn are lost in the shadows of time, but his origins and power base lay east of the river Conwy, and probably in Powys. The rise of his dynasty may have been facilitated by successful war against the Mercians and his family is closely associated with a stronghold at the former Anglo-Saxon burh of Rhuddlan. Although we lack reliable evidence, it is possible that Llywelyn himself had a base there by 1015.

The rise of Llywelyn coincided with a period of chaos and, most probably, civil war in Gwynedd. One of the few definitive pieces of information in the Welsh chronicle records that Cynan ap Hywel – a direct descendant of the Merfyn Frych dynasty – was 'slain' in 1003, and domestic strife seems to be the most likely explanation. A period of silence follows through to 1018, when it is recorded that Llywelyn killed a certain Aeddan ap Blegywryd and his four sons. Within four years the chronicle describes Llywelyn ranging widely across south as well as north Wales and he is accorded the title 'King of the Britons', an appellation that was reserved for the greatest rulers with the widest ambitions.

One important but disputed piece of evidence is available to shed further light on the rise of Llywelyn. The poem *Echrys Ynys* ('desolate the island') mourns the death of a ruler named Aeddan from Anglesey who led an army from Arfon (the region on the southern shore of the Menai Strait) to his final battle at Caer Seon. The battle site is on the west side of the Conwy, opposite Degannwy and close to the mouth of the river. Despite the fact that Ifor Williams favoured an eleventh-century date for the poem, both he and Kari Maund were reluctant to accept that the Aeddan in whose honour it was written could be connected with the Aeddan ap Blegywryd killed by Llywelyn. Charles-Edwards, however, disagrees, pointing out that no other known name fits the bill and that the poet treads a difficult path, being obliged to praise his former lord while having to take care not to upset the new regime under the control of Aeddan's conqueror.[5]

If we accept that *Echrys Ynys* was dedicated to Aeddan ap Blegywryd – and I see little reason to doubt this – it reinforces the idea that the power base of Aeddan's conqueror, Llywelyn, lay east of the Conwy. By contrast, Aeddan's court in Anglesey would connect him with the heartland of Gwynedd and the Irish Sea region, the core power base of what had become the northern branch of the Merfyn Frych dynasty. Aeddan is not named in the genealogies of the Merfyn Frych line, perhaps suggesting that civil strife had loosened its grip on power. Such upheaval may have opened the way for the leading dynasties of Powys to claim dominance over north Wales, a change that would ultimately help facilitate the rise of Bleddyn ap Cynfyn.

Rivalries following the death of Llywelyn ap Seisyll

Llywelyn died in 1023 and the sources for the years that follow remain sparse and unreliable. The little evidence we do have indicates that his death allowed the Merfyn Frych dynasty back on to the scene, although their rule was by no means uncontested. The dynasty had been split into two branches – northern and southern – since the time of Merfyn's grandsons in the early tenth century. The heartland of the northern branch was in Gwynedd, while that of the southern branch was in Deheubarth, in south-west Wales. At some point after Llywelyn's death, Iago ab Idwal of the northern branch was prominent on the political scene in Wales, while the brothers Maredudd and Hywel ab Edwin led the southern branch in Deheubarth.

There is no direct evidence that these two branches of Merfyn Frych's line worked together, but they do seem to have had common enemies in the other two dynasties prominent in Wales, whose leaders were Llywelyn's brother, Cynan ap Seisyll, and a former ally of Llywelyn, Rhydderch ab Iestyn, who was the dominant ruler of south-east Wales. Some of our most extensive evidence comes from the south-east in the form of the Book of Llandaff, a source that is notoriously difficult to interpret but is not necessarily unreliable. It states that, after the death of Llywelyn, Rhydderch was 'ruling over all Wales' except the island of 'Euonia', which is thought to be a reference to Anglesey.[6] This could mean that Iago ab Idwal was in control of the island and it may be speculated that Cynan was contending with him for power throughout the rest of north Wales.

Whilst little can be said with certainty about this bloody period, we know that Cynan was 'slain' in 1027. This may have been as part of a battle for control of the northern kingdom, but the Tudor historian David Powel claimed that the sons of Edwin from Deheubarth were responsible for Cynan's death. As with much other evidence on Wales that is unique to antiquarian sources, it is impossible to tell whether Powel had access to original material that is now lost to us, or whether he was simply making an educated guess to fill in blanks in his story. Rhydderch was killed in 1033 and again the perpetrators are unnamed, but the sons of Edwin are likely candidates. In 1034 Rhydderch's sons and the sons of Edwin fought each other at the battle of Hiraethwy, the location and result of which is unknown. In 1035, Maredudd ab Edwin was killed by the 'sons of Cynan'. This is thought to refer to the offspring of Cynan ap Seisyll, and their action could, perhaps, be seen as revenge for the killing of their father.

Gruffudd ap Llywelyn and the kingdom of Wales

If this version of events is far from being the only possible interpretation of the limited evidence, it at least ties in with the fact that the various texts of the Welsh chronicles only claim that Iago began to rule in the north – and the sons of Edwin in the south – in 1033, after the deaths of both Cynan and Rhydderch. Later historiography would see this as the return of the 'legitimate' Merfyn Frych dynasty to Gwynedd, but contemporary sources seem to have had no issue with the legitimacy of the rule of the likes of Rhydderch ab Iestyn and Llywelyn ap Seisyll, nor with that of their sons, who would dominate Wales in the middle decades of the eleventh century. Nothing more is known of the rule of Iago until its bloody ending in 1039 was recorded (without lament): 'Iago, king of Gwynedd was slain. And in his place ruled Gruffudd ap Llywelyn ap Seisyll; and he, from his beginning to the end, pursued the Saxons and the other Gentiles and slaughtered and destroyed them, and defeated them in a great number of battles. He fought his first battle at Rhyd-y-groes on the Severn, and there he prevailed. In that year he pillaged Llanbadarn and held rule over Deheubarth and he expelled Hywel ab Edwin from his territory.'[7]

We do not know who was responsible for the death of Iago, although the bloodied sword inevitably tends to be placed in the hands of the man who had the most obvious motive. This was, of course, his successor Gruffudd, the son of Llywelyn ap Seisyll. Having been born c. 1013, Gruffudd would have been a minor on the death of his father in 1023 and the only information we have on his early years comes from folklore. This suggests that an indolent youth turned into a restless, rampant, blood-drenched adolescent who became a feared presence on the Welsh political scene.[8] His cousins, the sons of Cynan, receive no mention after the reference to their killing of Maredudd ab Edwin in 1035 and – as no other male descendant of Llywelyn's father Seisyll is known – Gruffudd seems to have been the sole inheritor of the dynasty's claims to rule. This would have given him a formidable power base in Powys and after Iago's death – in whatever manner that came about – Gruffudd was soon recognised as king of north Wales. He was immediately strong enough to wage aggressive war and his power in Gwynedd and Powys did not waver until he found himself under overwhelming external pressure in the final months of his 24-year reign. This indicates that these two regions were essentially united and that his rule was considered legitimate.

Gruffudd used the strength and security offered by the backing of the northern realm to extend his dominion further. In the year of his accession he won a major engagement against his Mercian neighbours in the battle of Rhyd-y-groes, fought on Gruffudd's eastern border in the vicinity of Forden in the plain below Montgomery.[9] The relieving of pressure on this front enabled Gruffudd to turn west and south for an assault on the kingdom of Deheubarth, which was under the rule of Hywel ab Edwin. Gruffudd enjoyed immediate success and was soon ruling at least a portion of Deheubarth, but Hywel and the men of the south proved stubborn opponents who enjoyed significant support from Hiberno-Scandinavian fleets. Gruffudd eventually killed Hywel in 1044 in a battle fought at the mouth of the Tywi, a victory that left south-east Wales as the only part of the country outside the northern king's direct rule.

The dominant ruler in the south-east was Gruffudd's namesake, Gruffudd ap Rhydderch. His father, Rhydderch ab Iestyn, had been an ally of Llywelyn ap Seisyll and there is no hint of discord between the two families until 1045. In that year, chronicle records state that: 'There was great deceit between Gruffudd and Rhys, the sons of Rhydderch, and Gruffudd ap Llywelyn.'[10] The wording of this entry may suggest that the treachery was instigated by the sons of Rhydderch, and if this was the case they were to pay dearly for ending their alliance with Gruffudd ap Llywelyn. Having secured his position in south-west Wales, the northern king began looking east and south – the change in focus signalled by a raid on northern Herefordshire in 1052 – and the key to furthering his ambitions would prove to be an alliance with Earl Ælfgar of the house of Mercia. When the earl was exiled from England in 1055 he gathered a Hiberno-Scandinavian fleet which sailed to a rendezvous with Gruffudd ap Llywelyn at the mouth of the Wye. In the course of these events the northern king killed his southern namesake Gruffudd ap Rhydderch and conquered south-east Wales, before the allied force embarked on an expedition up the Wye valley that ended with the destruction of Hereford. Ælfgar was restored to his earldom and, after a protracted series of border skirmishes, Gruffudd secured acknowledgement of his kingship and territories in a peace treaty he concluded with Edward the Confessor in 1056.

Gruffudd had become the only native king to reign over all the lands that comprise modern Wales.[11] He had also extended the country, making significant conquests along the length of his eastern border to reclaim 'Welsh' lands that had been in Anglo-Saxon hands for centuries. Gruffudd was the outstanding leader of Wales in the middle ages and alongside him in his years of glory would have been his half-brother, Bleddyn ap Cynfyn.

2

Bleddyn's Rise to Power

The genealogies of Wales abound with references to Bleddyn ap Cynfyn, but he is the first of his line about whom anything definite can be said and – apart from the identity of his father – everything about his heritage is open to question. A genealogy in Mostyn MS 117, which was written in the last quarter of the thirteenth century, traces Bleddyn's lineage back to the legendary pre-Roman king of Britain, Beli Mawr.[1] In this source, Cynfyn's father is named as Gwerystan, his father as Gwyn, and Gwyn's father as Gwaithfoed. Most later genealogies omit the name of Gwyn from the family tree and make Gwerystan the son of Gwaithfoed. Yet even the name of Bleddyn's grandfather Gwerystan is somewhat uncertain; this is the form given in Mostyn MS 117, but *Brut (RBH)* has Gwerstan and the more common spelling in other genealogies is 'Gweystan'.[2] The name is thought to be a derivative of the English Werestan, suggesting that the origins and/or alliances of the family may have been connected with the Anglo-Saxon border and increasing the likelihood that the distinguished Welsh heritage that is claimed may be spurious. In contrast to the grand lists in the genealogies, the various versions of the Welsh chronicle only identify Bleddyn's father Cynfyn as the 'son of Gwerystan' and Kari Maund describes Bleddyn's forebears as 'little more than names in pedigrees'; we can learn no more about them.[3]

The pedigree compilers had good reason to record a glorious heritage for Bleddyn, whether it was real or fabricated. Gwerystan is thought to have had three children, Cynfyn, Ithel and Nest, but it was Cynfyn who would become the crucial piece in the genealogical jigsaw; he would be remembered as the ancestor of one of the five 'royal tribes of Wales' that were to become so important to the minor Welsh nobility of the succeeding centuries as they tried to insist upon their increasingly forlorn claims to glory, honour and respect.

If the early origins of Cynfyn's family are obscure, everything we learn of them in later years would suggest that their power base was in Powys. As suggested, the name Gwerystan could point to an English heritage, but other speculations are equally valid. It is possible that the family was long established in Powys, a noble clan that had offered its support to the descendants of Merfyn Frych during the years of overlordship that the Gwynedd dynasty enjoyed in north Wales. If there was an Anglo-Saxon connection, it could be that the family had cultivated alliances from across the border that may have helped them rise to prominence in the eleventh century. As will be seen, descendants of Cynfyn would be active near Llansantffraid-ym-Mechain in the later eleventh century, and an educated guess might place the family's heartlands in this region, to the north of Welshpool and close to the Anglo-Saxon border. To stretch the hypothesis even further, Llansantffraid-ym-Mechain – which has a settlement history dating back thousands of years, including Roman connections – is home to the high-status site of Plas-yn-Dinas. The ruins currently lack reliable interpretation but the context and setting suggest that the site may have been the stronghold of a noble line in this period.

Angharad ferch Maredudd

It seems certain that the family was prominent and well established by the time of the reign of Llywelyn ap Seisyll in the early eleventh century and it is likely that Cynfyn was an important supporter of that king. The key to the further elevation of the dynasty to a position that would eventually bring them the kingship occurred soon after Llywelyn's death in 1023, when Cynfyn married the king's widow, Angharad. She was a daughter of the important late-tenth century king of Wales, Maredudd ab Owain and, through him, had a direct connection to the Merfyn Frych dynasty, a connection that had helped bolster Llywelyn's claims to overlordship in the country. Such a distinguished marriage seems certain to have been a real coup for Cynfyn. The circumstances that brought him such a prestigious match can only be speculated upon, but Angharad and her young son Gruffudd – who is likely to have been about ten years old in 1023 – may have found themselves in a precarious position after Llywelyn's death. As discussed in the previous chapter, we can identify four prominent factions vying for control of Wales in 1023; they formed two alliances, Rhydderch ab Iestyn and Cynan ap Seisyll on one side, Iago ab Idwal and Maredudd and Hywel ab Edwin on the other. If Llywelyn's brother Cynan may seem a natural defender and supporter of Angharad and her son, it should be remembered that he would have had dynastic ambitions of his own, while his sons were active on the political scene. In such circumstances, Gruffudd ap Llywelyn's uncle Cynan may have been seen as the biggest threat to the youngster, prompting Angharad to seek security through marriage to a powerful noble from a line that would not threaten her young son's claim to kingship.

Cynfyn may already have had a partner and it can be seen that multiple wives were far from unusual in eleventh-century Wales; Bleddyn's son Cadwgan is known to have had at least five partners/ wives. Cynfyn's daughter Iwerydd is well attested in the records, but while the genealogies name her as Angharad's daughter, the Welsh chronicle accounts say that she was Bleddyn's half-sister, the daughter of Cynfyn by a different mother, and Kari Maund is inclined to accept this version.[4] There may also have been another sister called Nest; she is named in some pedigrees, but Maund considers the name to be fabricated in an attempt to trace certain dynastic lines back to Cynfyn.[5] The twelfth-century Herefordshire writer Walter Map also mentions a sister of Gruffudd ap Llywelyn,[6] but the context seems to suggest that she was older than her brother, meaning she was more likely to be Llywelyn's daughter than Cynfyn's. The only offspring that can be positively identified as the children of Cynfyn and Angharad were two sons, Bleddyn and Rhiwallon.

Bleddyn and Rhiwallon

We do not know when either son was born, but some suppositions can be made, starting with the likelihood that Bleddyn, who is always named first in our sources, was the elder brother.[7] Cynfyn married Angharad some time after Llywelyn's death in 1023, so it is highly unlikely that they had a child before 1024. In the extant records, Bleddyn and Rhiwallon are not mentioned until 1063, when they were already established on the political scene and capable of taking on the leadership of Wales after their half-brother Gruffudd ap Llywelyn's death. Given that Gruffudd himself was born c.1013 – and that he may have had an older sister – I would suggest that Angharad's prime child-bearing years were c.1010–35. This would suggest that both Bleddyn and Rhiwallon were born in the period c.1024–43, and I would tend to favour a date of c.1025–30.

If we try to refine this further, the age of the brothers at death can play no part in the calculations because both had their lives prematurely cut short, Rhiwallon in 1069 and Bleddyn in 1075. However, the activity of Bleddyn's offspring may provide some hints. The eldest of his known children may have been a daughter, Gwenllian, who was married to Caradog ap Gruffudd, the son of Gruffudd ap Rhydderch. I would suggest that this marriage was made as part of an alliance between Bleddyn and Caradog in 1065, or soon thereafter; the terminal date for the marriage is 1081, when Caradog was killed.[8] The earliest known activities of Bleddyn's sons occurred in 1088 when they were ruling and fighting on the Welsh political scene. This suggests that when Bleddyn was killed in 1075 none of them was in a position to contest the succession, possibly because they were minors. Two of his sons, Madog and Rhirid, were killed in the 1088 fighting, but Bleddyn's other known sons lived into the twelfth century, when all but one of them were killed by violence. Maredudd ap Bleddyn lived on, and is thought to have died of natural causes in 1132. An overview of these events could suggest that Bleddyn's eldest sons were not born until c.1060, which would seem rather late if Bleddyn himself was born in the 1020s. But Gwenllian was probably born earlier and numerous interpretations could be put on the evidence for Bleddyn's sons. For example, it is possible that he had other sons who had been born earlier, but that he secured a more advantageous marriage as he climbed the political ladder and that the offspring from this marriage were favoured in the later succession.

As already indicated, the first references to Bleddyn and Rhiwallon come in 1063, after the death of their half-brother. We can say nothing certain about their role while Gruffudd was forging his kingdom after 1039, but if a young Gruffudd had been raised with them in the household of Cynfyn and Angharad they are likely to have been well known to him. Walter Map's folk tales suggest that, when roused from 'the indolence of youth', Gruffudd 'left his father' and gathered a formidable band of ambitious warriors to his side.[9] If we accept this, the initial group that Gruffudd gathered into his *teulu* – his military household, composed of his most important nobles and most trusted warriors – is unlikely to have included the youngsters Bleddyn and Rhiwallon. In the years after 1039, Gruffudd and his followers won incredible victories, but these were achieved at heavy cost with bloody battles recorded against Hywel ab Edwin, Anglo-Saxon neighbours and Hiberno-Scandinavian raiders. As just one example, Gruffudd's final victory over Hywel and his Hiberno-Scandinavian allies in battle at the mouth of the Tywi in 1044 is recorded thus:

> And Gruffudd ap Llywelyn encountered him [Hywel]; and there was a mighty battle and many of the host of the foreigners and of his own host were slain at the mouth of the river Tywi. And there Hywel was slain and Gruffudd prevailed.[10]

Perhaps even more devastating to Gruffudd and his followers was the human cost of subduing the newly conquered lands of Wales. Ystrad Tywi would prove a particularly problematic area which was fiercely loyal to its own *uchelwyr*, the proud local nobility who could trace their own claims to kingship in the pedigrees and who looked for leadership to their own dynasties, such as that of Hywel ab Edwin. In 1047 it was recorded that 'about seven score men of Gruffudd ap Llywelyn's warband were slain through the treachery of the leading men (W. *uchelwyr*) of Ystrad Tywi'.[11] To lose 140 of his closest associates must have been a keen blow to Gruffudd and such a devastating loss is likely to have rocked his regime to its core. To have recovered in the way he did, the king would have needed to recruit new *teulu* members and to secure new sources of support, and it seems reasonable to speculate that Bleddyn and Rhiwallon could have gained promotion at this time to become leading deputies of Gruffudd's. This would have placed them at the heart of events through the most glorious years of Gruffudd's rule, which included the conquest of south-east Wales and the raids into Herefordshire that helped secure major territorial gains at the expense of Anglo-Saxon England. Such a role is likely to have brought the brothers into contact with the key political players in England and Wales, including the Welsh dynasties that Gruffudd had subdued, the nobles of Mercia and Harold Godwinesson and his leading men.

The fall of Gruffudd ap Llywelyn

The only source we have that alludes to the pre-1063 positions of Bleddyn and Rhiwallon is late and obscure. The chronicle of Pierre de Langtoft was written in Yorkshire in the late thirteenth or early fourteenth century and reads as follows in its description of Harold's 1063 campaign against Gruffudd:

> Gruffudd has two brothers, the king [Edward the Confessor]
> Wishes to conciliate them.
> Bleddyn and Rhiwallon, so I heard them named,
> They were accustomed to support the king's part
> In all the wars which Gruffudd raised;
> Therefore the king caused them to be
> Enfeoffed in his lands,
> And he took their homages of them.[12]

This could be read as suggesting that Bleddyn and Rhiwallon had always sided with Edward in his wars against Gruffudd, or that they had always sided with Gruffudd. There are examples in this period of Anglo-Saxon rulers endowing dispossessed Welsh nobles with lands in England and using these exiles as political leverage against incumbent Welsh leaders, but this seems unlikely to have been the situation with Bleddyn and Rhiwallon. Although their family may have enjoyed local prominence in Powys, without the support of Gruffudd they would have lacked a claim to the overall kingship of Wales. After Gruffudd's death, our sources imply that the two brothers were accepted as the leaders of Powys and Gwynedd and that they had some sort of claim to overlordship in other parts of the country, although rival claims still existed. It is hard to see how two exiles, who had played no part in Gruffudd's regime, who were little known within Wales and who owed their position entirely to English sponsorship, could establish effective control. However, within two years they were strong enough to turn against the Anglo-Saxon king to whom, according to Langtoft, they had paid homage in 1063, which suggests that their kingship relied on more than English patronage.

A more likely scenario would seem to be that the brothers had worked their way into prominent positions of power during Gruffudd's regime and that in 1063 the Anglo-Saxons made a concerted effort to win over their support. Up until this point Gruffudd had, of course, seemed impervious to any Anglo-Saxon attempts to control him; as he rose to dominance in Wales he had defeated, even humiliated, his Anglo-Saxon enemies every time they clashed. But a number of events in the late 1050s and early 1060s weakened the Welsh king and prepared the way for his downfall. In 1059 the Welsh chronicles record the death of Owain ap Gruffudd, who is believed to have been Gruffudd's son, and quite possibly his eldest son and intended heir.[13] The king's other sons may have been minors, a situation that could have awakened the ambitions of other nobles in Wales, perhaps including Bleddyn and Rhiwallon. With Gruffudd ageing and his conquests over, the king's ability to keep his leading men happy with the distribution of land, booty and other forms of largesse was restricted.

The most significant rupture of his power base occurred in late 1062 with the death of his most important ally, Earl Ælfgar of Mercia.[14] The alliance with Ælfgar had been the foundation of Gruffudd's extended kingdom of Wales, a friendly Mercia meaning that the rich lowlands of his exposed eastern border were free from the threat of attack. The combined power of Wales and Mercia counter-balanced the power of the house of Godwine, which dominated most of the rest of England. In this political climate, it seems unlikely that Harold Godwinesson – a known enemy of Ælfgar – could have succeeded Edward the Confessor on the English throne, as his ambitions would have been blocked by the Welsh-Mercian alliance. But Ælfgar was succeeded by his young, inexperienced son Edwin, opening a window of opportunity for Harold to strike, claim victory over Gruffudd and engineer the situation that would eventually bring the house of Godwine to the throne of England.

Ælfgar's death may have occurred at Edward's Christmas court in Gloucester in 1062; it was from the Christmas court that Harold launched a lightning raid on Rhuddlan with the intention of slaying Gruffudd. The Welsh king got away by boat, but could not stop Harold from burning his palace and fleet. The earl returned to England to prepare a major spring offensive against Gruffudd, gathering a naval force at Bristol while his brother, Tostig, moved a land force from Northumbria against north Wales. John of Worcester has one of the fullest accounts. He was a cleric writing on the Welsh border in the early twelfth century and – whilst his work agrees with the facts laid out in the *Anglo-Saxon Chronicle* – it also furnishes additional detail from other sources and local traditions:

> About Rogationtide [25–8 May] [Harold] set out from Bristol with a
> naval force, and sailed around a great part of Wales. His brother Earl
> Tostig met him with mounted troops, as the king commanded, and they
> at once joined forces, and began to lay waste that region. By that the
> Welsh were coerced, and gave hostages.[15]

As Harold sailed around the south Wales coast the lands that Gruffudd
had fought so hard to subdue quickly sided with the invader. Soon
representatives of the dynasties that Gruffudd had displaced were
again ruling in south-east and south-west Wales; it may be speculated
that they had been in Harold's entourage, or that they were already
ruling in Wales under Gruffudd's overlordship but quickly shed their
allegiance to him when Harold arrived on the scene. Soon after the
invasion Caradog, the son of Gruffudd ap Rhydderch whom Gruffudd
ap Llywelyn had killed in 1055, was ruling as the dominant king in
the south-east from his base in Upper Gwent. The Tudor historian
David Powel claimed that Harold entered south Wales in 1063 'by
the procurement of Caradoc ap Gruffyth ap Rytherch, and others'.[16]
Caradog's cousin, Rhydderch ap Caradog, may well have been a part
of the alliance; after 1063 he held dominion in Lower Gwent and
Ewias with a royal centre at Caerleon, while Cadwgan ap Meurig of
the ancient line of Glamorgan held a position of power further west.
In Deheubarth, three nephews of Gruffudd's old rival Hywel ab Edwin
– the brothers Maredudd, Hywel and Rhys ab Owain – enjoyed rule
after Harold's campaign.

The inability of Edwin and Mercia to support Gruffudd meant
that the lowlands of the king's exposed eastern border were rendered
indefensible against Tostig's attack in the north and all that was left
to him was his original power base, Powys and Gwynedd. Yet, despite
the apparently hopeless situation he was facing, an account in the *Life
of King Edward (Vita Ædwardi Regis)* would suggest that Gruffudd
fought a vigorous, rearguard guerrilla campaign as he tried to resist
the formidable enemies lining up against him:

> [Gruffudd] sought remote retreats.
> Inured to lurk in distant dikes, from which
> He can with safety fly upon the foe,
> Exploiting barren lands with woods and rocks,
> He galls the brother earls with drawn-out war.[17]

But despite such resistance Harold and Tostig – both outstanding military commanders – proved relentless, methodically grinding down opposition in a manner that left a lasting impression. The professionalism of the campaign, its effectiveness and its comprehensive result were remembered in detail by the twelfth-century writers Gerald of Wales and John of Salisbury and it has even been suggested that Harold's plan to subdue Wales was used as a blueprint by the country's eventual conqueror, Edward I, in the later thirteenth century. Gerald presents this graphic account:

> [Harold] advanced into Wales on foot, at the head of his lightly clad infantry, lived on the country, and marched up and down and round and about the whole of Wales with such energy that he 'left not one that pisseth against a wall'.[18]

It is at this point in the war – with Harold and Tostig using their superior resources to wear out the desperate Welsh defence – that I would place Pierre de Langtoft's account of the defection of Bleddyn and Rhiwallon to the English side.

Submission and succession

If the unfaithfulness of Gruffudd's subjects in south Wales had been somewhat predictable, the loss of his half-brothers' support would have been a mortal blow to the king. John of Worcester says that the Welsh 'surrendered, and promised that they would pay [Harold] tribute, and they deposed and outlawed their king Gruffudd'.[19] This indicates that Gruffudd fought on with a handful of his closest companions – probably his *teulu* – even after Bleddyn, Rhiwallon and his other key allies had gone over to Harold and repudiated his authority. The Welsh chronicle accounts suggest that Gruffudd conducted his guerrilla resistance from 'the waste valleys'; this would seem to fit with the king having made a logical retreat to his most formidable citadel, the natural stronghold of Gwynedd Uwch Conwy, to the west of the Conwy and in the mountainous heartland of Snowdonia. In such circumstances, Bleddyn and Rhiwallon may have been left to lead the resistance in Powys where, recognising the hopelessness of Gruffudd's situation, they had come to a negotiated agreement with Harold. Gruffudd fought on to the bitter end, the *Anglo-Saxon Chronicle* recording:

In autumn King Gruffudd was killed on 5 August by his own men because of the fight he fought against Earl Harold. He was king over all the Welsh, and his head was brought to Earl Harold, and Harold brought it to the king, and the figurehead of his ship and the ornaments with it. And King Edward entrusted the country to the two brothers of Gruffudd, Bleddyn and Rhiwallon, and they swore oaths and gave hostages to the king and the earl, promising that they would be faithful to him in everything, and be everywhere ready on water and on land, and likewise would pay such dues from that country as had been given before to any other king.[20]

The manner of the succession of Bleddyn and Rhiwallon to the kingship would have an enormous impact on the entire course of their reigns and it needs to be considered from both the English and the Welsh perspective. Their succession has also had a considerable influence on the way in which modern writers have viewed their roles and their positions in history. John Edward Lloyd was somewhat dismissive of the brothers:

Harold did not conquer Wales in the sense in which this was done by Edward I, or even obtain the hold upon the country which was acquired by Henry I. What he achieved was the reduction of the Welsh question from one of national importance to its old status as a mere border difficulty. New rulers were placed in power; Bleddyn and Rhiwallon, the sons of an unknown Cynfyn ap Gwerystan by his wife Angharad, the widow of Llywelyn ap Seisyll, submitted to Harold and from him received Gwynedd and Powys, swearing to be faithful to King Edward in all things and to pay all renders which in the past had been yielded to the English crown. [Lloyd then describes the various rulers established in south Wales in 1063]. From none of these new men was there reason to fear attacks on the grand scale, such as had made the late leader so formidable, but they were under no greater restrictions than the predecessors of Gruffudd ap Llywelyn, and had it in their power to harass the marches no less persistently than in the days of yore.[21]

Lloyd felt it was significant that Bleddyn 'had no claim to rule on the score of his birth' and this view seems to have influenced later historians.[22] To Rees Davies, Bleddyn and Rhiwallon were 'puppet rulers installed by Edward the Confessor in north Wales on his own terms'.[23] Roger Turvey has written extensively on the Merfyn Frych dynasty, which returned to prominence in Wales in the twelfth century, and he seems to see Bleddyn and Rhiwallon as usurpers who delayed the coming to power of Gruffudd ap Cynan, the forefather of the later princes of Gwynedd and Wales:

> As the son of Cynan and grandson of Iago, Gruffudd had a good claim to the throne of Gwynedd [in the 1060s and 1070s] but his way was blocked by the two half-brothers of Gruffudd ap Llywelyn, namely Bleddyn and Rhiwallon, sons of Cynfyn. Although Bleddyn and Rhiwallon were, like their half-brother Gruffudd, usurpers with no real claim to rule in Gwynedd other than by conquest, they were powerful enough to keep their nobility in check. Gruffudd had to bide his time and in 1075 the death of Bleddyn ap Cynfyn, following that of his brother Rhiwallon in [1069], gave him the opportunity to press his claim to Gwynedd.[24]

It is important, though, to consider more contemporary views of Bleddyn and Rhiwallon within Wales, as these give little indication that there was unease associated with the 'right to rule' of the two brothers. The various versions of the Welsh chronicle are extremely positive in their descriptions of Gruffudd ap Llywelyn. They contain almost no information on the details of the final campaign against him, neglecting even to mention English involvement and concentrating on the 'treacherous' aspects of the king's downfall:

> Gruffudd ap Llywelyn was slain, after innumerable victories and taking of spoils and treasures of gold and silver and precious purple raiment, through the treachery of his own men, after his fame and glory had increased and after he has aforetimes been unconquered, but was now left in the waste valleys, and after he had been head and shield and defender to the Britons.[25]

Blame for the 'treachery' does not seem to fall on Bleddyn and Rhiwallon, however, and Bleddyn in particular gets very positive treatment whenever he is mentioned in the three surviving Welsh-language versions of the chronicle; his noble and humane characteristics are repeatedly praised. A lament for Bleddyn under the year 1078 lauds him as

> the gentlest and most merciful of kings; and he would do no harm to anyone unless injury were done to him, and when injury was done, it

was against his will that he would avenge the injury; he was gentle towards his kinsmen and a defender of orphans and of the weak and widows, and the strength of the learned and the honour and foundation of the churches, and the comfort of the lands, and generous towards all; and terrible in war and lovable in peace, and a defence for all.[26]

Care does, of course, need to be taken with such chronicle entries. Bleddyn would have had the chance to curry favour with the clerical authors in the course of his reign and the records were subject to amendment in the years after his death. This fact is particularly pertinent when dealing with the Welsh-language versions of the chronicle, the three of which – *Brut (Pen. 20)*, *Brut (RBH)* and *Bren.* – will be collectively referred to as the *Brutiau*. In the late eleventh and early twelfth centuries the *Brutiau* take on a greatly expanded form, containing much material that is absent from the surviving Latin versions of the chronicle, which are referred to collectively as *Annales Cambriae*. While *Annales Cambriae* was composed at St Davids in this period, Kari Maund and David Stephenson have established that the source behind the expanded *Brutiau* entries was associated with Llanbadarn Fawr.[27] Furthermore, Stephenson notes that, in the period 1091–1163, the deaths of members of the family of the renowned Welsh cleric Sulien were 'scrupulously recorded' in the *Brutiau*. As a result, he makes a convincing case for seeing Daniel ap Sulien – whose death was recorded in 1127 – as the driving force behind the expanded version of the chronicle. The *Brutiau* are notably favourable in their treatment of Bleddyn and his family, a fact that may have much to do with twelfth-century political realities, when Bleddyn's descendants were supporters of the clerical community (W. *clas*) at Llanbadarn Fawr. It may also have had something to do with history; I would speculate that the establishment of the *clas* that Sulien belonged to at Llanbadarn Fawr was associated with Gruffudd ap Llywelyn's attack on the church in 1039, an event that may have seen the displacement of the previous *clas*. The major interests of the *Brutiau* can be associated with a wide kin group whose common ancestor seems to have been Gruffudd's mother, Angharad. This resulted in favourable treatment of Angharad's father, Maredudd ab Owain; her husband, Llywelyn ap Seisyll; her son by Llywelyn, Gruffudd; her son by Cynfyn, Bleddyn; and her descendants through Bleddyn into the twelfth century. Possibly Gruffudd had appointed a close relative of Angharad as the head of the Llanbadarn Fawr *clas* in 1039.

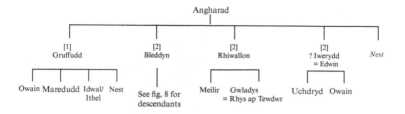

[1] Denotes children of Angharad's marriage to Llywelyn ap Seisyll (d. 1022)
[2] Denotes children of Angharad's marriage to Cynfyn ap Gwerystan
Names in italics are of doubtful provenance
Iwerydd was a daughter of Cynfyn's, but perhaps not by Angharad

Figure 3 The known descendants of Angharad ferch
Maredudd ab Owain

Whether as the result of bias or not, there is no sense of unease in either *Annales Cambriae* or the *Brutiau* with regard to the 'legitimacy' of Bleddyn or Rhiwallon. In fact, neither the brothers nor the political situation in Wales are mentioned in the years between the death of Gruffudd ap Llywelyn and 1069. As discussed below, Gruffudd's sons were killed in battle against Bleddyn and Rhiwallon in that year.[28] Rhiwallon was also killed in the fight, after which Bleddyn was said to rule in north Wales and Maredudd ab Owain in the south. Looking for signs of political bias in these chronicle entries can be dangerous, but if they suggest anything, it seems to be support for the 'legitimacy' of the sons of Gruffudd ap Llywelyn; they do not, in any way, suggest support for the 'legitimacy' of Gruffudd ap Cynan.

Whatever the opinion of the chroniclers of south-west Wales, it seems clear from the power they wielded that Bleddyn and Rhiwallon were accepted as the rulers of Powys and Gwynedd in 1063, and likely that they retained some sort of ambition with regard to the wider overlordship over the rest of Wales that had been enjoyed by their half-brother. While they are likely to have tried to push claims to such overlordship to their maximum extent, the 'kings' in the rest of the country – especially those in south-west and south-east Wales – would have seen things very differently. The additional complicating factor was the position that Bleddyn and Rhiwallon found themselves in with regard to the king of England. The *Anglo-Saxon Chronicle* is clear on the fact that the brothers owed their position of power to

Figure 4. Llanbadarn Fawr. The chroniclers of Llanbadarn Fawr showed
notable interest in, and favour to, Bleddyn and his descendants

Edward the Confessor, and the silence of the Welsh chronicles in this
regard could be deliberate and convenient. The kings of south-west
and south-east Wales would also have known how the northern rulers
had come to power and – as fellow adherents of Harold in the 1063
campaign – would have been reluctant to accept any claims to overlordship from the new rulers of Powys and Gwynedd. It is notable
that Bleddyn and Rhiwallon get no mention in any surviving source
from south-east Wales; in contrast, the Book of Llandaff was keen
to use the renowned reputation of Gruffudd ap Llywelyn to boost
Llandaff's claims to authority, describing him as 'King Gruffudd,
sole and pre-eminent ruler of the British'.[29]

There was a long tradition by which Welsh kings submitted to ultimate English overlordship, but there were degrees of submission and
the humiliating terms imposed on Bleddyn and Rhiwallon were at the
extreme end of the scale. The first point to note is that the English
sources never refer to the brothers as kings, a snub that stands in stark
contrast to references to Gruffudd; he was always acknowledged as
King of Wales in surviving sources from England, Ireland and even

continental Europe. As noted, the *Anglo-Saxon Ch*ronicle records that in 1063:

> King Edward entrusted the country to the two brothers of Gruffudd, Bleddyn and Rhiwallon, and they swore oaths and gave hostages to the king and the earl, promising that they would be faithful to him in every-thing, and be everywhere ready on water and on land, and likewise would pay such dues from that country as had been given before to any other king.

This needs to be contrasted with the peace treaty that Gruffudd forced on Harold and Edward c.1056, when he was at the height of his powers following his successful border wars and with his unshakeable alliance with Ælfgar in place. The *Anglo-Saxon Chronicle* attempts to gloss over this peace, merely noting that 'Gruffudd swore oaths that he would be a loyal and faithful underking to King Edward', but the nature of the agreement needs to be considered more closely.[30] Walter Map has a story of a meeting between Gruffudd and Edward which took place on the England-Wales border, on an old ferry crossing near the present site of the original Severn Bridge road crossing. Although the tale was open to embellishment by its author and is not verified by any other source, it fits with the political situation in 1056 and – as a Herefordshire man – Map would have been well placed to gather local knowledge about such an encounter.

> In the midst of [Gruffudd's] works of wickedness there is one thing he is recorded to have done nobly and courteously. In his time he was so oppressive and obnoxious to his neighbours that it became necessary for Edward, then king of England, either to use entreaty on behalf of his subjects, or take up arms in their defence. Ambassadors were sent from both sides and then they negotiated from opposite banks of the Severn, Edward being at Aust Cliff, [Gruffudd] at Beachley. The nobles went to and fro between them in boats, and after many exchanges of messages, the question was long debated which of them ought to cross over to the other. It was a difficult crossing owing to the roughness of the water, but that was not the ground of the dispute. [Gruffudd] alleged his precedence, Edward his equality: [Gruffudd] took the ground that his people had gained all England, with Cornwall, Scotland, and Wales, from the giants, and affirmed himself to be their heir in a direct line: Edward argued that his ancestors had got the land from its conquerors. After a great deal of quarrelsome contention Edward got in a boat and

set off to [Gruffudd]. At that point the Severn is a mile broad. [Gruffudd] seeing him and recognising him cast off his state mantle – for he had prepared himself for a public appearance – went into the water up to his breast and throwing his arms lovingly about the boat, said: 'Wisest of kings, your modesty has vanquished my pride, your wisdom has triumphed over my foolishness. The neck which I foolishly stiffened against you you shall mount and so enter the territory which your mildness has today made your own.' And taking him on his shoulders he seated him upon his mantle, and then with joined hands did him homage. This was an admirable beginning of peace, but, after the Welsh manner, it was only kept till they felt able to do mischief.[31]

Although Gruffudd was said to acknowledge his position as an under-king, there was little else about his position that could be called subservient. The very location of the meeting was telling; the western side of the ancient ferry crossing had been left in Welsh hands when Offa's Dyke was constructed as the border in the eighth century, but by the eleventh century Beachley was usually in English hands. That it was in Welsh hands in 1056 is indicative of the extensive border conquests that had been made by Gruffudd and formally acknowledged in the peace treaty. Edward conceded to Gruffudd 'all the lands beyond the river called Dee'.[32] Domesday Book confirms the scale of Gruffudd's conquests, which reversed centuries of Anglo-Saxon expansion before and after the construction of Offa's Dyke. John Edward Lloyd noted that English westward expansion had continued after the building of the dyke, with settlements like Edderton, Forden, Thornbury, Woodliston and Hopton in the region of Montgomery, and, further south, the likes of Waterdine, Weston, Pilleth, Radnor, Burlingjobb, Kington and a group of villages on the north bank of the Wye around Eardisley. Such areas, and many others along the entire length of the Wales-England border, are recorded as 'waste' in Domesday Book, many yielding no dues to the English exchequer as late as 1086. This indicates the extent of Gruffudd's conquests, some of which may have been made before 1056, but were confirmed by the treaty of that year.[33]

Other than the broad acknowledgement of Edward's overlordship, which would have been accompanied by solemn oaths, there seem to have been no practical concessions made by or restrictions placed on Gruffudd. He does not seem to have had to give hostages, pay dues or offer any military service. Such public acknowledgement of the

Figure 5. Beachley. The ancient ferry crossing at Beachley is where Gruffudd ap Llywelyn is said to have agreed his peace deal with Edward the Confessor

prestige of his kingship would have been invaluable, as it seems reasonable to speculate that Gruffudd had used propaganda regarding Wales's subservience to England to help fuel his rise to this position; Map's reference to Gruffudd tracing his heritage back to those who had conquered Britain 'from the giants' would suggest this. Herefordshire is likely to have been significant in any propaganda campaign; it had been at the heart of the border wars, with Gruffudd claiming territorial and ecclesiastical control of Archenfield, a region of southwest Herefordshire which had very strong Welsh attachments. The area had been at the centre of conflict between Anglo-Saxons and Welsh for centuries for both practical and symbolic reasons. Perhaps most tellingly, King Athelstan, arguably the most domineering of all Anglo-Saxon kings in his dealings with Wales, had compelled nearly all the kings of Wales to gather at his court in Hereford c.930. This resulted in an agreement that the Wye would be the boundary between English and Welsh in the region and, according to the twelfth-century writer William of Malmesbury, Athelstan imposed humiliating terms on the under-kings. This was said to have included an enormous annual tribute of 20lbs of gold, 300lbs of silver, 25,000 oxen and large numbers of hounds and hawks, while the underling status of the Welsh was underlined repeatedly as they attended Athelstan's courts and put their names to his charters. This degradation of the status of Welsh kingship has been suggested as the catalyst for the composition of the poem *Armes Prydein*, a rallying call that pictured the gathering of a grand alliance of the Welsh, the Irish, the Scots, the Danes of Dublin and the Britons of Cornwall, Brittany and Strathclyde. This great force was to overcome Athelstan and drive the hated 'Saxons' out of the country.[34]

From the perspective of Edward and Harold, the treaty they imposed on Bleddyn, Rhiwallon and Wales in 1063 would have been regarded as a return to the accustomed order of things; the reference to the payment of 'such dues from that country as had been given before to any other king' may even allude to the settlement imposed by Athelstan in the previous century. The open-ended promise to 'be everywhere ready on water and on land' further emphasised the fact that the new Welsh kings were to be at the beck and call of their English masters. The deal was accompanied by huge territorial gains for England at the expense of Wales, reversing Gruffudd's achievements and leaving a legacy that would pave the way for future conquests. The views of twelfth-century writers may be seen as telling; the Anglo-Norman chronicler Geoffrey Gaimar says that 'no heed was paid to the Welsh' after the death of Gruffudd and John of Salisbury claims that Harold established a law after 1063 whereby any Welshman found with a weapon beyond the dyke would be deprived of his hand and 'thereby the strength of the Britons was so impaired by the Duke that almost the entire nation seemed to die out and their women were married to Englishmen by the indulgence of the king.'[35] While Bleddyn would always strive to recreate the kingdom of Wales that had been built by Gruffudd, the obvious reduction in status that had accompanied his rise to the throne would hinder his ambition, thwarting him practically and in terms of propaganda as he tried to claim dominion over other 'kings' in the country.

3

The New Kings

The unenthusiastic light in which the succession of Bleddyn and Rhiwallon has been seen by contemporary historians has been noted and is exemplified in this analysis by Rees Davies:

> Within Wales itself [Gruffudd ap Llywelyn's] death left a vacuum of authority and power. His hegemony had been founded on military might and personal dependence; it had no institutional base which could outlast his own downfall. The natural fissiparousness of Welsh 'political' life – if such a genteel term may be used for the litany of family and inter-dynastic conflicts, raids, kidnappings and murders – now reasserted itself. Puppet rulers (such as Bleddyn and Rhiwallon ap Cynfyn, installed by Edward the Confessor in north Wales on his own terms), political exiles (notably Maredudd ab Owain of the dynasty of Deheubarth and Gruffudd ap Cynan of the former dynasty of Gwynedd), and adventurers (such as Trahaearn ap Caradog in north Wales and Caradog ap Gruffudd in south Wales) competed desperately with each other and joined forces in a perplexing kaleidoscope of temporary alliances to further their ambitions. Rarely, even by its own standards, was the Welsh 'political' scene more fluid, its allegiances more brittle and its supremacies more short-lived than in the later eleventh century.[1]

Such a broad picture of the scene helps make accessible what can, indeed, seem like a 'perplexing kaleidoscope', but I have contended elsewhere that such a dismissive view of the nature of Gruffudd ap Llywelyn's kingship should be questioned[2] and the rule of Bleddyn and Rhiwallon also needs to be looked at in more detail.

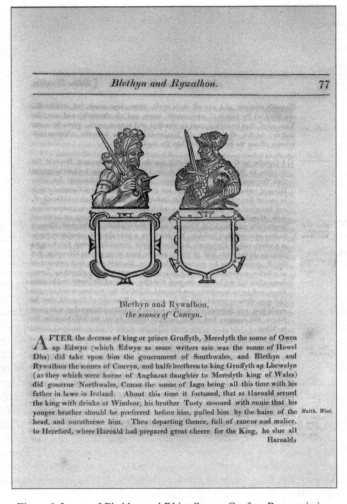

Blethyn and Rywalhon.   77

Blethyn and Rywalhon,
the sonnes of Convyn.

AFTER the decease of king or prince Gruffyth, Meredyth the sonne of Owen ap Edwyn (which Edwyn as some writers saie was the sonne of Howel Dha) did take vpon him the gouernment of Southwales, and Blethyn and Rywalhon the sonnes of Convyn, and halfe brethren to king Gruffyth ap Lhewelyn (as they which were borne of Angharat daughter to Meredyth king of Wales) did gouerne Northwales, Conan the sonne of Iago being all this time with his father in lawe in Ireland. About this time it fortuned, that as Haroald serued the king with drinke at Windsor, his brother Tosty mooued with enuie that his yonger brother should be preferred before him, pulled him by the haire of the *Matth. West.* head, and ouerthrewe him. Then departing thence, full of rancor and malice, to Hereford, where Haroald had prepared great cheere for the King, he slue all
Haroalds

Figure 6. Image of Bleddyn and Rhiwallon ap Cynfyn. By permission of Llyfrgell Genedlaethol Cymru / The National Library of Wales. The earliest known attempt to depict Bleddyn and Rhiwallon, from David Powel, *The Historie of Cambria, now called Wales* (London, 1584). The woodcuts had been used in other books to depict different characters and can have no claim to be an accurate historical depiction of the brothers.

One of the questions that cannot really be addressed is the nature of the relationship between the two brothers. We simply lack the evidence to determine whether there was some sort of joint kingship, whether one brother was regarded as superior and/or whether one brother ruled in Powys and the other in Gwynedd, but some educated guesses can be attempted. What can be said is that there is no evidence of the brothers ever being in conflict with each other; when the pair are mentioned in our sources they always appear to be working harmoniously with the same goal in mind. I have suggested that the fact that Bleddyn is always named first could indicate that he was the elder brother, and perhaps this hypothesis could be stretched further to suggest that he was regarded as the superior ruler. To look more closely at the country as a whole, let us consider the political situation in the various, loosely defined regions of Wales in 1063.

NORTH WALES

Powys

As already discussed, from the ninth century onwards Powys and Gwynedd must be regarded as one kingdom and this remained true for the rest of Bleddyn's life. However, there were distinct regional identities within the kingdom and it is important to remember that, although Gwynedd had originally played the dominant role, the ruling dynasties had been Powys families for most of the eleventh century. Given the suggestion that Bleddyn was the senior of the two brothers in the kingdom, it is possible that he based his rule on the family heartlands in Powys and that Rhiwallon was handed more responsibility in Gwynedd. Support for this theory may be suggested by the fact that a certain Cynwrig ap Rhiwallon was exercising authority in Gwynedd at the time of Bleddyn's death in 1075. However, as discussed below, the identity of Cynwrig is uncertain; he may have been Bleddyn's nephew, or he may have been an important member of another prominent Powys dynasty, that of Tudur Trefor.

After 1063 Powys was a greatly diminished and weakened territory when compared to the one that had been ruled by Gruffudd ap Llywelyn. Gruffudd had used his alliance with Mercia to help him expand eastwards into the rich lowlands of the border, the extent of his acquisitions being revealed in the 1086 Domesday Book survey.

A key plank in Bleddyn's strategy would be to recreate his half-brother's Mercian alliance by supporting Ælfgar's son Edwin, but the young Edwin's position in 1063 cannot be determined with certainty. While Gruffudd's downfall had greatly weakened the strategic position of Mercia, Edwin had profited territorially and he was ruling directly over lands that had previously been held by his father's ally. These included Rhuddlan, where Gruffudd had had an important court and naval base; it may even have served as some sort of 'capital' for his kingdom.[3] It is thought that Rhuddlan and Bistre had been secured by the Welsh earlier in the eleventh century, possibly by Llywelyn ap Seisyll in the troubled second reign of Æthelred II (1014–16).[4] Llywelyn's son Gruffudd took things to the next level after 1056, securing Exestan and the hidated part of Atiscros. In an analysis of the region of Tegeingl, Thomas Charles-Edwards says that 'to judge by Domesday, Gruffudd ap Llywelyn had ruled north-east Wales, old Mercian territory, from the 'burh' at Rhuddlan almost to the gates of Chester.'[5] In its description of Maelor Cymraeg hundred, Domesday Book states: 'King Edward gave to King Gruffudd all the land that lies beyond the river called Dee. But when King Gruffudd wronged him, he took this land from him and gave it back to the Bishop of Chester and to all his men, who had formerly held it.'[6] Rhuddlan is described thus:

> Before 1066 Englefield lay there; it was all waste. Earl Edwin held it. When Earl Hugh acquired it it was likewise waste. Now he has in the lordship half of the castle called Rhuddlan, which is the head of this land. He has there eight burgesses; half of the church and the mint; half the iron mines, wherever found in this manor; half the waters of the Clwyd; of the mills and fisheries made there, namely on the part of the river that belongs to the Earl's holding; half of the forests which did not belong to any other village of this manor; half of the toll, and half the village called Bryn. Land for three ploughs. They are there, in lordship, with seven slaves.[7]

Further south the evidence is more difficult to interpret, but Charles-Edwards suggests that Llywelyn had also claimed land in Shropshire, including Whittington, Maesbury and Chirbury; the three manors are said in Domesday Book to have paid the *firma* of half a night in the time of Æthelred, the nature of the reference suggesting that this was the last time the English were able exact revenue from those lands. The area around Hen Domen/Montgomery also provides an interesting case study. This was in the region where Gruffudd had won his famous victory at Rhyd-y-groes and he seems likely to have enjoyed control of this area, but in 1066 it was being used as a hunting ground by three Anglo-Saxon thegns.[8] Yet, despite such territorial losses in the east, Powys remained a powerful and wealthy realm and a region that would be the key resource for Bleddyn as he sought to build his position in the rest of the country. The extent of its southern and western borders are difficult to determine exactly and will be considered in the following sections.

Gwynedd

The strength of the union between Powys and Gwynedd has been stressed, but Harold's strategic campaign against Gruffudd ap Llywelyn had touched on the fault lines that existed in the relationship between the Welsh regions and reawakened interest in the area from across the Irish Sea. The Hiberno-Scandinavian influence on both north-west and south-west Wales had been huge since the ninth century and, while this has generally been viewed with regard to their raiding, ravaging and slave-taking, it extended deep into the areas of settlement and political control. For example, David Wyatt has noted that the Hiberno-Scandinavians were making increasing claims to overlordship over parts of Britain at this time, and that they had a particular interest in Anglesey, which could serve as a staging point on the important route between Viking settlements in Dublin, the Wirral and York.[9] As one indication of the extent of their influence, archaeological excavation has uncovered a major, heavily defended Viking trading settlement at Llanbedrgoch on Anglesey, close to Aberlleiniog castle, that is thought to date to the tenth century. The proximity of such an alien, fortified, high-status site just sixteen miles from the traditional seat of power in Gwynedd at Aberffraw has led to speculation that it was part of a Viking takeover of Anglesey.[10] Such Viking activity came at the time when the Merfyn Frych dynasty ruled in Gwynedd, Powys and Deheubarth, and it has been noted that Merfyn himself is thought to have come from the Isle of Man and may have used military support from the Irish Sea region to establish his family in Wales.

Gruffudd ap Llywelyn had fought bitter wars over many years against Hiberno-Scandinavian enemies and Ireland had proved a key source of support for his rivals within Wales. The foundering of a fleet from Ireland that was heading to Wales in 1052 seems to have finally ended that threat and freed Gruffudd's hand to concentrate on his plans for expansion into Anglo-Saxon territory. The strength of the king had brought Viking raids on Wales to an end and no attacks are recorded in the period 1052–73. But the fact that political powers across the Irish Sea retained an interest in Wales can be seen from the fact that they harboured Cynan ab Iago of the Merfyn Frych dynasty. Cynan was the son of the king of Gwynedd whom Gruffudd ap Llywelyn had succeeded, Iago ab Idwal. He was exiled to Dublin after his father's death and the ruling Scandinavian dynasty there – the Silkenbeards – proved accommodating. Cynan married a Silken-beard heiress named Rhanillt who was both the daughter and grand-daughter of kings of Dublin, and antiquarian sources suggest that the exiled Welsh noble may have helped lead the Hiberno-Scandinavian fleets that troubled Gruffudd in 1041 and 1052.

Cynan then disappears from view and was so little known in Wales that when his son Gruffudd emerged on the Welsh political scene he was known as 'grandson of Iago' rather than 'son of Cynan'. But Harold gathered together all the opposition to Gruffudd ap Llywelyn for the 1063 campaign and he also had a close connection to Cynan's protector, the king of Dublin Diarmait mac Máel na mBó. Diarmait had helped Harold when he was exiled from England in 1052 and would harbour the last Anglo-Saxon king's sons after his death at Hastings in 1066. In 1063 it seems likely that Cynan established himself in part of Gwynedd – most probably Anglesey – with military support from Ireland, and that from this position he played a part in the assassination of Gruffudd ap Llywelyn.[11] Two related Irish chronicles – *The Annals of Ulster* and *The Annals of Loch Cé* – say that Gruffudd was slain by a 'son of Iago', while another less well-known Irish source, found in British Library MS Add. 30512, actually names Cynan ab Iago as Gruffudd's killer. One later source, the twelfth-century *History of Gruffydd ap Cynan*, states that Cynan was a king of Gwynedd and, while this title was not generally recognised, it is possible that he was able to secure some sort of spurious claim to the position in the confused summer of 1063. Using a base in Anglesey, it is con-ceivable that Cynan could have contacted members of Gruffudd's inner entourage in their final redoubt in Snowdonia. The *Anglo-Saxon Chronicle* is clear on the fact that Gruffudd was betrayed and killed by 'his own men' – suggesting his inner household – and the various versions of the Welsh chronicle dwell on the 'treachery of Gruffudd's

own men'. Cynan – perhaps using dynastic and/or personal connections to his father Iago, and perhaps fuelling rivalries that existed
between the ruling elites of Gwynedd and Powys – may have been
able to engineer the betrayal and murder of Gruffudd.

If this was the case, however, it is striking that the return of this
'legitimate' claimant to the throne, who enjoyed significant external
military support, seems to have made no lasting impact in Gwynedd.
No more is heard of Cynan and, as has been mentioned, when his
son appears on the Welsh political scene with Hiberno-Scandinavian
support after the death of Bleddyn, he was identified as 'grandson
of Iago' rather than 'son of (the unknown) Cynan'. Nor were any
Viking raids on Wales recorded until 1073, although after this date
Hiberno-Scandinavian fleets were again to have a major impact on
the Welsh political scene. Despite the strains put on the relationship
between Powys and Gwynedd in 1063, it seems that Bleddyn and
Rhiwallon were able to drive any external pretenders from Gwynedd,
counter any threats from across the Irish Sea, win over or destroy
any Gwynedd dynasties of uncertain loyalty and secure their rule
over the area. Perhaps this securing of the region even included the
slaying of Cynan. Gwynedd, like Powys, would be a key source of
power and support for Bleddyn for the rest of his reign as he sought
to further his ambitions elsewhere in Wales.

MID WALES

Ceredigion

The independence of Ceredigion as a kingdom had ended in the ninth
century when it was conquered by Rhodri Mawr, the son of Merfyn
Frych. In the succeeding centuries, control of the area would be contested between the rulers of Gwynedd-Powys and the leaders of Deheubarth. After his accession in 1039, for example, one of Gruffudd ap
Llywelyn's first recorded actions was to march west from his successful
battle at Rhyd-y-groes into Ceredigion to attack Llanbadarn Fawr,
the opening move in his campaign to destroy Hywel ab Edwin and
conquer Deheubarth. While Gruffudd was able to eliminate Hywel's
main dynastic line, other branches of the family survived and these
claimed power in Deheubarth in 1063. They would have undoubtedly
harboured ambitions to rule in Ceredigion, but it seems most likely

that in 1063 they were restricted to Dyfed and Ystrad Tywi in the south-west, the areas where Hywel and his supporters had been most deeply entrenched. Bleddyn and Rhiwallon are likely to have been in control of Ceredigion in 1063 and the northern rulers would have seen the area as just another part of their kingdom.

Rhwng Gwy a Hafren

Rhwng Gwy a Hafren (between Wye and Severn) has an erratic history as an independent territorial entity. The region roughly equates to modern Radnorshire and there are indications that it existed as a kingdom in its own right in the early middle ages, but that any independent status ended in the tenth century.[12] The territory was part of Gruffudd ap Llywelyn's kingdom of Wales, suggesting that he had either displaced an important local dynasty descended from a nobleman called Elystan Glodrydd, or had come to some accommodation with members of that family. Elystan's son Cadwgan was part of a dynastic line that was to re-establish an element of independence for Rhwng Gwy a Hafren in the twelfth century, but Cadwgan's activities are otherwise unknown. Following Bleddyn's death in 1075, Cadwgan's sons – Llywelyn and Goronwy – fought the battle of Camddwr against Bleddyn's killer, Rhys ab Owain.[13] This may suggest that they had been subjects of Bleddyn and a supportive part of his power structure.

Brycheiniog

The position of Brycheiniog in the east of south-central Wales may be seen as analogous to that of Ceredigion in the west. The region's status as an independent kingdom seems to have ended in the tenth century with competition for control coming from Gwynedd-Powys and the rulers of south-east Wales, added complications being the interests of leaders from across the Herefordshire border and from Deheubarth. Gruffudd ap Llywelyn devoted particular attention to the area in his border wars and can be connected with events in the region of Llangors and Glasbury. Bleddyn and Rhiwallon may have seen Brycheiniog as a part of their dominion in 1063, although they would have felt pressure on their borders from Harold Godwine. Perhaps even more significant was the position of Caradog ap Gruffudd in the region. As argued below, he was a long-term ally of Bleddyn, and part of the deal that secured this partnership may have been an acknow-ledgement of Caradog's right to rule in Brycheiniog. This agreement may even have extended to allow Caradog an influence in parts of Rhwng Gwy a Hafren.

SOUTH WALES

While the dominion of Bleddyn and Rhiwallon extended over a large proportion of the country, the situation in south-east and south-west Wales was more complicated. The English had 'entrusted' Wales to the two brothers after Harold's campaign of 1063, but the earl had also allied with the traditional ruling dynasties of south-east and, perhaps, south-west Wales, who sought power in their families' heart-lands. If Bleddyn and Rhiwallon believed they had some sort of claim to overlordship over these regions, it is unlikely that the local rulers shared this view. The brothers' submission to the humiliating terms imposed by Harold would have also diminished their prestige and distanced them from any claims that Gruffudd ap Llywelyn had made to the kingship of all Wales. As noted, the various versions of the Welsh chronicle make no mention of Bleddyn until 1069 and even then it is stated that he only held Powys and Gwynedd, with leadership of Deheubarth explicitly denied to him. But the fact that some sort of claim to overlordship did exist is suggested by the career of Bleddyn's son Cadwgan, the most powerful native Welsh leader in the late eleventh century whose first recorded act was a raid on Deheubarth in 1088. Kari Maund notes that at least part of Cadwgan's claim to rule was inherited from his father and that 'at the height of his authority, Cadwgan's interests seem to have ranged from Eifionydd, Ardudwy and Penllyn in the north to Cydweli in the south; for much of his life he apparently controlled most or all of Powys, together with Cere-digion, and, perhaps, part of Meirionydd and Eifionydd.'[14]

Deheubarth

The likelihood that Bleddyn and Rhiwallon were ruling Ceredigion in 1063 has been discussed, but the position in the rest of Deheubarth is uncertain. Caradog ap Gruffudd may have had some part to play, but three brothers who were the nephews of Gruffudd ap Llywelyn's old enemy, Hywel ab Edwin, would also have had an interest. These were Maredudd, Hywel and Rhys ab Owain, with Maredudd – who may have been the eldest – holding the senior position; the Welsh chronicle evidence says that he started to rule Deheubarth in 1069. The brothers, part of the Merfyn Frych dynasty, may have enjoyed political and military backing from across the Irish Sea. The exact situation in 1063 cannot be determined with certainty but there would seem to be three possible scenarios. The first would be that the brothers were ensconced in their family's homelands in Deheubarth under the rule of Gruffudd ap Llywelyn and that they took the opportunity presented by Harold's invasion to increase their power and autonomy; in the second scenario, they would have been exiles in England in 1063, harboured by Harold and brought back as part of his invasion plan; the third possibility is that they had been in exile in Ireland and were able to return, in 1063 or soon afterwards, with Hiberno-Scandinavian support. In the years to come they would look to expand their power into south-east Wales, Brycheiniog and Rhwng Gwy a Hafren, but at this time they seem restricted to south-west Wales. Gower – traditionally a contested border territory between Deheubarth and Glamorgan – was probably beyond their reach. A reference in the Book of Llandaff suggests that the rulers of Glamorgan may have pushed their territorial ambitions further, claiming dominion even to the west of Carmarthen. It is stated that 'King Meurig reigned in Glamorgan as far as the ford of the trunk on Tywi', but it must be remembered that this was in the context of a claim by Llandaff for ecclesiastical control in the region.[15] Meurig was probably dead by 1063 and it may be signifcant that the source does not claim that his son Cadwgan ruled so far west.

South-east Wales

The situation in south-east Wales was even more confused. As in Deheubarth, there seem to have been three main contenders but – unlike Deheubarth – the three came from competing dynastic lines which all sought dominance over wider territories. To complicate matters, Harold held land on the eastern border and would look to follow his successful 1063 campaign with further territorial encroachments. A variety of sources suggest that rebellion in south Wales led by

Caradog ap Gruffudd was the prelude to the 1063 invasion. Caradog was the son of Gruffudd ap Rhydderch, the formidable king of south-east Wales, who had been killed in 1055 by Gruffudd ap Llywelyn with the help of Ælfgar and a Hiberno-Scandinavian fleet. In the years after 1063 Caradog, based in Upper Gwent, was a powerful influence, but another noble is associated with rule in Lower Gwent about this time, Caradog's cousin and sometime rival, Rhydderch ap Caradog. Caradog ap Gruffudd's activities at Portskewett in 1065 (discussed below) indicate that he at least had an interest in Lower Gwent, but Rhydderch seems to be in control of this region *c.*1067. Further west in Glamorgan was yet another ruler claiming the title of king: Cadwgan ap Meurig. I have suggested elsewhere that Glamorgan was the most autonomous region of Wales under the rule of Gruffudd ap Llywelyn and that Cadwgan and/or his father may have retained a position of authority under Gruffudd's dominion.[16] In 1063, it may have been that the rulers of the region quickly saw the need to rally to Harold's side, or alternatively Cadwgan may have been another exile who was able to return to his family's heartlands on the back of the earl's invasion.

As discussed below, at some point in the period 1063–5 Harold had a falling out with Caradog and may have attempted to supplant him with Maredudd ab Owain from Deheubarth. Caradog fought back and *c.*1067, according to the Book of Llandaff, was ruling Gwynllŵg, Upper Gwent and Ystrad Yw, with Rhydderch in Lower Gwent and Ewyas, and Cadwgan exercising power in Glamorgan.[17]

Bleddyn's kingship

A shortage of evidence for this period means that it is all too easy to dismiss the nature of the rule of the leaders of the day as unsophisticated. As has been seen, Rees Davies claimed that Gruffudd ap Llywelyn's kingship 'had no institutional base which could outlast his own downfall' while Roger Turvey saw Bleddyn and Rhiwallon as little more than usurping conquerors of Gwynedd who 'were powerful enough to keep their nobility in check'. Contemporary sources, however, seemed to see more in the kingship of the day, as in this description of Bleddyn's rule from *Brut (RBH)*'s entry for 1078:

[He] was the gentlest and most merciful of kings; and he would do no harm to anyone unless injury were done to him, and when injury was done, it was against his will that he would avenge the injury; he was gentle towards his kinsmen and a defender of orphans and of the weak and widows, and the strength of the learned and the honour and foundation of the churches, and the comfort of the lands, and generous towards all; and terrible in war and lovable in peace, and a defence for all.[18]

The core of Bleddyn's power would undoubtedly have been the military household (W. *teulu*) that accompanied him on his tours around his realms, but there was much more to his rule than *force majeure*, as can be seen from an examination of some of the key institutions of government.

The maerdrefi

Welsh leaders of the day divided their lands into hundreds (W. *cantrefi*) and/or the smaller division known as the commote. The Welsh laws give a standardised model of the way such divisions worked, but in reality the arrangements would have been more ad hoc. What we can see, though, is that these large land divisions were then split into manors and townships and the manors would include the leader's main administrative centre, known as the *llys*, and his *maerdref* ('home farm'). A Welsh king would travel between his *maerdrefi* while on circuit (W. *cylch*) of his domain, supporting himself and his household from the produce of the lands and taking the other dues that were owed to him. Given the nature of the 1063 succession, I would suggest that Bleddyn and Rhiwallon were able to exploit their rule in this way throughout Gwynedd, Powys, Ceredigion, Rhwng Gwy a Hafren and, perhaps, Brycheiniog, but not in deepest Deheubarth or southeast Wales. Even if there was an accepted claim to overlordship in these areas, it is unlikely that the local rulers would have willingly allowed the northern kings to make a due-collecting *cylch* around the *maerdrefi* of the south. In order to impose such a direct form of overlordship, Bleddyn and Rhiwallon would have needed a major show of military force.

There is still archaeological work to do to uncover these early Welsh *maerdrefi*. As many were on strategic sites associated with administration and rule, their locations were reused by future generations.[19]

In Gwynedd, for example, the early Norman invaders built some of their early earthwork castles on top of old *maerdref* sites.[20] The sort of high-status sites we should consider when looking for Bleddyn and Rhiwallon's main residences and administrative centres could include Llanbadarn, Dinas Emrys, Bangor, Aberffraw, Abergwyn-gregyn, Degannwy, Cwrt Llechryd and Talgarth (Brycheiniog).[21] As suggested, the brothers' family may have had a special connection with the Llansantffraid-ym-Mechain region, and the nearby high-status site of Plas-yn-Dinas would bear further investigation.

Naval strategy

Given the geography of the country and the difficulty of travel, a naval strategy was vital for any medieval ruler with ambitions to rule all of Wales. Gruffudd ap Llywelyn is one of the few Welsh rulers of the period about whom we can say anything in this regard; he seems to have had the resources to maintain an effective fleet and to have used *maerdrefi* sites that were accessible from the sea to keep in touch with – and keep control of – his lands throughout the country.[22] Gruffudd would have faced formidable rivalry and competition on the waves from both his Hiberno-Scandinavian enemies and his Anglo-Saxon foes. It is notable that one of the more triumphalist notes sounded from England after Harold's 1063 campaign was the fact that Gruffudd's naval ambitions had been comprehensively overthrown:

> They [Harold and Tostig] smashed a fleet – for Welsh control and lore
> Was not the equal of the Ocean's chiefs –
> And take a prow and stern of solid gold,
> Cast by the smith's assiduous skill, and this
> With looted treasures and the hostages,
> As proof of victory they give their king.[23]

There is no evidence to suggest that Bleddyn and Rhiwallon tried or had the ability to recreate the naval presence that Gruffudd had been able to maintain at the height of his power. Rhuddlan, where Gruffudd had maintained a strong naval presence, was never ruled by the brothers, nor was the rest of the north Wales coast between the Clwyd and the Dee. While it seems probable that they used the

sea to travel between their coastal *maerdrefi* in north Wales and Ceredigion, the lack of a more formidable navy is likely to have diminished
their ability to exert their power and influence further into south Wales.
Towards the end of Bleddyn's reign in 1073 we see the mounting of
the first recorded Hiberno-Scandinavian attack on Welsh shores since
1052, and after his death in 1075 his successor Trahaearn's inability
to control the sea lanes between Anglesey and Rhuddlan would cause
the new leader major difficulties.[24]

Administration and the church

Unfortunately there are no surviving charters featuring Bleddyn or
Rhiwallon, a fact that limits any discussion of their administration.
However, the positive descriptions of Bleddyn in the *Brutiau* would
suggest that – like other contemporary rulers – he was a patron of the
church and would have made use of clerical resources in his administration and for propaganda purposes. Each *maerdref* tended to have
a church associated with it and Bleddyn and Rhiwallon would have
used the abilities of clerics at all levels. Surviving evidence from the
more important religious centres can help us consider some of the
major churches within their realms whose resources would have been
utilised within the kingdom.

In Gwynedd, there are two names, Dyfan and Revedun, associated
with leadership of the church in Bangor at this time, but the names
are all we know and nothing more can be said of them. We know
even less about Clynnog Fawr, but it was prominent in the struggle
for control of Gwynedd that followed Bleddyn's death in 1075, a fact
that seems indicative of its importance.[25] In Ceredigion, as suggested
above, the clerical family at Llanbadarn Fawr, headed by the famous
scholar Sulien (1011–91), would seem to have been supporters of
Bleddyn and of his sons and successors into the twelfth century, with
Sulien's son Daniel perhaps the man behind the positive treatment
of the dynasty in the *Brutiau*. Sulien became bishop of St Davids in
the course of Bleddyn's reign and control of the resources and propaganda power of the great church there would have played a vital part
in the battle for the rule of Deheubarth.[26]

To turn to churches in Powys, the position of St Asaph in Bleddyn's
reign is more obscure; according to legend the church was founded
in the sixth century, but its history can only be securely traced to the

mid twelfth century. There is, however, plenty of circumstantial evidence to suggest that the church was an important prop to Gruffudd ap Llywelyn's regime; St Asaph is just three miles south of Gruffudd's court at Rhuddlan and the later ecclesiastical boundaries of the diocese can be closely equated with the border conquests made by the Welsh king. The only known reference to an eleventh-century bishop of St Asaph – a man named Melan of Llanelwy – is dated to *c.* 1070, but this comes from a document of 1145 from St Davids, the reliability of which cannot be guaranteed. It must also be remembered that the fall of Gruffudd left Rhuddlan and the surrounding territory in Anglo-Saxon hands, limiting the value of St Asaph to Bleddyn and Rhiwallon.

Whatever the position of St Asaph, the most important church in Powys in the early middle ages is thought to have been Meifod. Bleddyn's grandson built a new church there in the twelfth century, around the time he constructed the nearby castle of Mathrafal, but Meifod was a *clas* church and a place of pilgrimage from at least the tenth century. After his death in 1137, Gruffudd ap Cynan arranged multiple bequests to churches; only two Welsh churches outside Gwynedd were honoured, Meifod and St Davids. David Stephenson has linked the creation of Meifod's famous stone slab with Daniel ap Sulien and the *clas* from Llanbadarn Fawr, suggesting that the context may have been the clerical family's retreat from Llanbadarn after the Norman conquest of Ceredigion.[27]

Bleddyn ap Cynfyn and Welsh law

The importance placed on the contribution of learned clerics in Bleddyn's regime is most clearly indicated by the significant impact that his reign had on the development of Welsh law.[28] The codification and standardisation of this law is traditionally attributed to Hywel Dda (d. 950) and Bleddyn is one of only two rulers associated in the lawbooks with changes, the other being the twelfth-century ruler of Deheubarth, Rhys ap Gruffudd (the Lord Rhys, d. 1197). Such a reputation as a reformer could lend further credibility to the fulsome elegy for Bleddyn from *Brut (RBH)* cited above, which echoes the memory preserved of the law's codifier as Hywel 'the Good'. Perhaps such a reputation is also reflected in a poetic description of Bleddyn contained in the *Ecclesiastical History* of Orderic Vitalis, which says he was a 'handsome' or 'fine' king (L. *pulchro*).[29] The fact that the changes in the law are specifically attributed to Bleddyn and that no mention is made of Rhiwallon may lend credence to the possibility that Bleddyn was the senior ruler or, perhaps, may indicate that he had more opportunity to devote himself to administrative affairs in the later years of his reign, after his brother's death in 1069.

Figure 7. Depiction of a Welsh king on his throne holding a sceptre, from the law book known as *Peniarth 28*. By permission of Llyfrgell Genedlaethol Cymru / The National Library of Wales.

The surviving manuscripts and fragments of Welsh law were originally the working books of lawyers, used to record information which
they found useful.[30] Apart from five versions in Latin, the lawbooks
were written in Welsh and form three broad families, or redactions.
None of the surviving manuscripts are identical, but neither are any
of them entirely different from the others, meaning that there are
frequent digressions and additions, even within each redaction. Significant references to Bleddyn as a legal reformer are found in five sections
of the redaction known as Llyfr Iorwerth, the most developed form
of the laws that is associated with thirteenth-century Gwynedd; there
are no such references in Llyfr Cyfnerth – which is regarded as the
earliest, most primitive redaction – nor in early versions of Llyfr
Blegywryd, a redaction that has been associated with Dyfed. The fact
that his memory was preserved in this Gwynedd text is significant,
given the fact that the thirteenth-century princes of that region came
from a dynasty that had supplanted Bleddyn's descendants, who were
restricted to Powys. Although there was intermarriage between the
dynasties of Gwynedd and Powys in the twelfth century, there was
also significant rivalry and conflict. Linking legal reforms to Bleddyn
would not have redounded to the glory of the later Gwynedd dynasty,
increasing the likelihood that they were included when Llyfr Iorwerth
was compiled because they could reliably be attributed to him.

Of the five references in Llyfr Iorwerth, two are in the earlier, less
complete version associated with Llywelyn ab Iorwerth (d. 1240) and
the other three in the later Llyfr Colan.[31] Of the two earlier Llyfr
Iorwerth mentions, the first deals with land reform:

> Sharing of Land. It is free at all times to share land (unless the right to
> the share is denied, though the season be closed). Thus it is right for
> brothers to share land amongst them: four acres to each *tyddyn* ('toft')
> – and after that Bleddyn ap Cynfyn changed it to 12 acres for the *uchelwr*
> and eight for the *aillt* and four for the *godaeog*; and yet it is soundest
> that the toft is four acres.[32]

The text's editor, Dafydd Jenkins, notes that a *tyddyn* would imply a
plot of land carrying a house, but the laws make it clear that some
tyddyn land had no buildings on it; he suggests, therefore, that 'perhaps
the essential feature of the *tyddyn* was that the land was enclosed'.
An *uchelwr* was a free notable in Welsh society, while the *aillt* and
godaeog were of client status; the difference may imply that a *godaeog*

was unfree, although over time the distinction between a *godaeog* and an *aillt* seems to have become blurred. Huw Pryce notes that the passage is problematic because unfree classes would not be expected to divide land; it would be divided for them as *tir cyfrif* by the *maer* or steward of the bond township. Whatever the technicalities of the issue, the ruling associated with Bleddyn would seem to be aimed at introducing an innovation that drew a distinction between different classes when it came to inheritance. The concluding sentence stating that the original ruling was 'soundest' may suggest that the reform did not work, or perhaps that the specific reason that it was implemented by Bleddyn was no longer relevant; it seems that the compiler did not consider it to be correct law. However, Bleddyn was clearly remembered as a reformer of the law and this is emphasised in other references to him in the legal texts.

The other early Llyfr Iorwerth reference to Bleddyn is a small part of a larger section on theft that deals with issues including compensation and punishment:

> In the law of Hywel there was payment and second payment for stolen property; and thereafter Bleddyn ap Cynfyn changed it, so that it was enough to pay the person his loss according to his own appraisal. Let his own goods go as he wishes, if he has no children; if he has children he is not entitled to bequeath anything except the church's *daered*, and his debts.[33]

Such a ruling in favour of victims would seem to be in keeping with Bleddyn's reputation in the *Brutiau* as a 'defender of the weak'. It may be speculated that in this regard Bleddyn's reign contrasted with the harsher rule of his predecessor, Gruffudd ap Llywelyn, something that may have helped people in Wales to warm to Bleddyn after Gruffudd's subjects turned against him in the final months of his reign. It is difficult to push such a suggestion too far, as we have no direct evidence for Gruffudd's intervention in legal matters. However, his expansionist regime is likely to have been resource-hungry and one of the folk tales about the king written by Walter Map in the twelfth century may be revealing. He tells the story of Gruffudd's jealousy with regard to his 'very beautiful wife'. The king is said to have been enraged when he heard that a young nobleman had dreamt of having an affair with her. After threatening the youth with torture and death, Gruffudd refused the customary offering of themselves as security by the man's clan and threw him in jail, demanding retribution. The matter was turned over to a legal expert – 'a man preeminent in such dealings' – who ruled that:

> We must follow the laws of our land, and can by no means annul what our fathers ordained and what has been established by long use. Let us then follow them and not produce anything new until a public decree directs us to the contrary. It has been promulgated in our oldest laws that he who outraged the consort of the King of Wales should pay 1,000 kine to the king and go free and unharmed. With regard to the wives of princes, and every class of magnates in like manner, a penalty was appointed according to the rank of each, with a certain number specified. This man is accused of dreaming that he abused the queen and does not deny the charge. Had the offence confessed been real, it is certain that 1,000 kine would have to be paid. In respect that it is a dream, we adjudge that this young man shall set 1,000 kine in the king's sight on the bank of the lake in Behthen [Llangors], in a row in the sunlight, that the reflection of each may be seen in the water, and that the reflections shall belong to the king, and the kine to him who owned them before, inasmuch as a dream is the reflection of the truth. This decision was approved by all and ordered to be put in execution, in spite of the angry protests of [Gruffudd].[34]

Such a tale could, perhaps, be related to a memory of Gruffudd's rule and his need for resources, which saw him push every legal right to its limits, however dubious the grounds. The case for such an interpretation is strengthened by the tale's setting at Llangors in Brycheiniog, an area which was at the heart of Gruffudd's border wars of 1055–6 and would have facilitated easy transmission of stories to Walter Map in Herefordshire.

To turn to the Llyfr Colan references to Bleddyn, the later thirteenth-century manuscript is described by Dafydd Jenkins as a revised edition of the Iorwerth redaction in which tractates have been reworded more concisely, sometimes amended, and often supplemented from another source.[35] The first reference to Bleddyn relates to compensation for corn damage and the second to compensation for pigs, sheep, goats, geese and hens.[36] In both instances, the passage is exactly the same as in the earlier Llyfr Iorwerth text, save that the later Llyfr Colan versions attribute the reforms to Bleddyn; no mention is made of who was responsible for the change to traditional law in the earlier text. The final reference to Bleddyn in Llyfr Colan serves to emphasise further his reputation as a merciful reformer, as it limits the cases of theft that merit a sentence of execution; again, the same section is included in the earlier Llyfr Iorwerth text, but there the law change is not attributed to a particular person.[37]

Bleddyn also gets a mention in a mid-fourteenth century text, NLW Peniarth MS 35 (G):

> The law of Hywel is, whoever shall offer property to a lord for law as to land and soil, is, although he shall lose the land, to pay the property he promised to the lord: Bleddyn, however, caused the payment to be made by the one who should have the land; and we mostly do thus at present. However, the alteration by Bleddyn was not a law, but a good regulation; for there is but one law, according to the Cymry, for causes, to wit, that of Hywel.
>
> If a person says that there are two laws, the law of Hywel and the law of Bleddyn, and call for one of them, and the judge adjudge according to the other; he can give his pledge against the judge as judging wrong, since he named the law, and he [the judge] adjudged according to the other.[38]

The explicit division between the law of Hywel and that of Bleddyn is intriguing, with the compiler also casting doubt on whether Bleddyn's changes should be regarded as law, or as good ordinance. Despite this categorisation, it is implied that either version may be valid and can be appealed to by the plaintiff. While this may only be the hypothetical legal argument of the compiler of the lawbook which was used to train prospective lawyers, it shows the persistence of the idea of Bleddyn as a legal reformer and the authority that his name could command; his ordinances were potentially of equal weight with the law of Hywel, even if their status could be challenged.[39]

While there are no references to Bleddyn in early versions of Llyfr Blegywyryd, he is named in relation to a rule in a late, much-extended version of Blegywyryd which derives from Cardiganshire; the mid fifteenth century MS, BL Add. MS22356 (S):

> If he be found the third time in the country, after being banished, according to the law of Hywel, he is to have his limb cut off, whatsoever person he may be: nevertheless, Bleddyn, son of Cynfyn, altered this; to wit, that he was to be executed.[40]

This entry seems unique in the law reforms attributed to Bleddyn in that it imposes a harsher punishment; execution rather than loss of limb.[41] Overall, however, the legal texts would seem to offer some support to the *Brutiau*'s picture of a ruler of good character, ability and authority who inspired respect and even, perhaps, affection in his subjects.

Immediate family of Bleddyn and Rhiwallon

Many of the most important followers, military supporters and clerical and other administrative officers during the regime of Bleddyn and Rhiwallon would have been related to the brothers. The heritage of the pair has been considered and the innumerable references to the dynasty in the genealogical material touched upon. Part of the reason for these multiple references can be found in developments in later twelfth-century Powys, where a bewildering multitude of nobles who could proudly trace their descent from Bleddyn found themselves competing for power and status in a politically fragmented land.[42] Although such men depended on royal status for their position they were also likely to be the victims of royal power, which meant that it was 'only natural for such men to express present grievance through an appeal to the memory of past kings'[43]. It is not proposed to analyse every branch of the family tree in detail, but an attempt can be made to discuss Bleddyn's closest relatives.

To consider his siblings first, Bleddyn's sister Iwerydd (a daughter of Cynfyn, but probably not by Angharad) receives significant attention in the genealogies. She married a man named Edwin and their sons, Uchdryd and Owain, were prominent on the political scene in the late eleventh and early twelfth centuries, Uchdryd being involved in repeated conflicts with the sons of Bleddyn.[44] One pedigree gives Bleddyn a second sister, Nest ferch Cynfyn, but Kari Maund doubts her existence, believing Nest to have been created as a way of tying other Powys dynasties to the important figure of Bleddyn. The known, surviving children of Gruffudd ap Llywelyn, the half-brother of Bleddyn and Rhiwallon, played important roles in the reign of their uncles, and Maredudd, Idwal and Nest will be discussed below. One genealogical tract suggests that Gruffudd had another son, Cynan, the child of a woman named Ceinfryd, but nothing more is known about him.[45]

We know much less about Rhiwallon than we do about his brother and co-ruler, Bleddyn; in fact, their sister Iwerydd receives much more attention in the genealogies than Rhiwallon. A certain Cynwrig ap Rhiwallon was killed in 1075 in the immediate aftermath of Bleddyn's death as part of an assault on the surviving regime in north Wales; opinion is divided on whether Cynwrig was Bleddyn's nephew or a more distant relation, a Powysian noble from the well-known dynasty of Tudur Trefor.[46] Meilir ap Rhiwallon, who is thought to have been a nephew of Bleddyn, enters the historical record earlier than any of his uncle's offspring when he is found fighting – and dying – on the side of Bleddyn's successor, Trahaearn, at the battle of Mynydd Carn in 1081.[47]

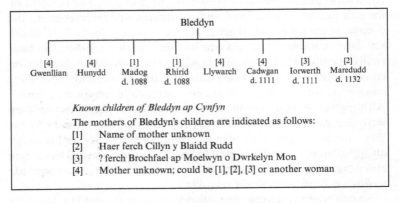

Figure 8 Bleddyn's wives and children

To turn to Bleddyn, one reason for his later prominence in the genealogies is simply the size of his immediate family; we can name at least six sons (Madog, Rhirid, Llywarch, Cadwgan, Iorwerth and Maredudd) and two daughters (Hunydd and Gwenllian). The names of Bleddyn's partners or wives are obscure, but there were at least three separate mothers; Madog and Rhirid are said to have had the same (unnamed) mother, while Iorwerth's mother is said to have been the daughter of a man named Brochwel. Maredudd's mother is the only woman to whom we can attach a name; Haer, the daughter of Cillyn y Blaidd Rudd. We do not know whether any of these three women was also the mother of Llywarch, Cadwgan, Hunydd or Gwenllian. We also have an intriguing reference to a concubine of Bleddyn's, 'a beautiful woman named Dylad';[48] given his obvious appetites, we may speculate that she was not his only mistress.[49]

The possibility that Gwenllian was Bleddyn's eldest child has been discussed and is supported by her marriage to Caradog ap Gruffudd. Owain Wan, the son of Gwenllian and Caradog, was killed in 1116, the evidence for this coming from an extended entry in the *Brutiau* that has him allied with two of his cousins; Owain and Maredudd, the sons of Hunydd by her marriage to Rhydderch ap Tewdwr (the brother of Rhys). No other known offspring of Bleddyn would seem to have been old enough to play a prominent role in Bleddyn's reign. His rise to the kingship might have opened the way to marriage with a daughter of one of the leading noble lines in Powys, and it is possible that the known sons of Bleddyn who were active on the political scene came from this and later dynastic alliances, while Gwenllian was the product of a less prestigious marriage made in his earlier years. The earliest record of the activities of his sons comes in 1088 when Madog, Cadwgan and Rhirid led an assault on Rhys ap Tewdwr in Deheubarth. They were initially successful and forced Rhys to flee to Ireland, but he returned with military support to defeat the brothers in battle, killing Madog and Rhirid. Cadwgan was probably the most significant native leader in north Wales in the 1080s and 1090s and he survived until 1111, when both he and his brother, Iorwerth, were slain in the civil feuding that tore Powys apart. Llywarch is not mentioned in the chronicles and the only significant fact we know about him is that he was married to a daughter of Gruffudd ap Cynan. Maredudd, who seems to have died of natural causes in 1132, did not really come to prominence until 1111. He fathered at least four sons and it was from this line that the most important native rulers of later twelfth- and thirteenth-century Powys emerged.

It is of particular importance to note the name of one member of Bleddyn's extended family, Trahaearn ap Caradog, the man who would succeed to power after his death.[50] Trahaearn is usually referred to as Bleddyn's 'cousin', but although he was clearly a kinsman, he was probably not a first cousin. No exact definition of their relationship can be given, but it has been suggested that Trahaearn's mother was Cynfyn's sister or, alternatively, that the connection was through a sister or cousin of Bleddyn's mother, Angharad.[51] We have no references to Trahaearn during the reign of Bleddyn, but it must be assumed that he was an important noble who was likely to have been at the king's right hand. The position of Trahaearn seems indicative of the extended kinship groups that formed the ruling elite in the kingdom of north Wales and, more particularly, in Powys in the mid to late eleventh century. Many, perhaps the majority, of the elite could trace a blood relationship to Bleddyn, Rhiwallon and Trahaearn. While most of their names are lost to us, in the years after Bleddyn's death we have references to Cynwrig ap Rhiwallon, Gwrgenau ap Seisyll, the sons of Rhys Sais, and Goronwy and Llywelyn ap Cadwgan;[52] all of them had important roles in Trahaearn's regime and all are thought to have been his kinsmen.

4

Anglo-Saxons, Vikings and Normans

If Bleddyn and Rhiwallon found themselves in a position of significant but restricted power within Wales in 1063, it is clear that from the outset of their rule they sought a wider dominion. Their ambition may well have matched that of their half-brother, Gruffudd ap Llywelyn and, like him, their only route to achieving their aim was through successful alliances with men of power and influence across the English border. The brothers' way forward may have seemed obvious; they had been elevated to prominence by Harold, the most powerful nobleman in Britain and it is likely that Harold would have seen the value of an agreement with the Welsh leaders. The close relationship between Gruffudd and Ælfgar had caused him extreme discomfiture in the 1050s and a similar alliance for himself could only have furthered his ambition to claim the crown of England. But any deal with Harold would have been on his terms and he was a domineering ruler, as his encroachments in south-east Wales were to show. Although the peace treaty of 1063 had brought Bleddyn and Rhiwallon to power, it was also a source of humiliation to the brothers and to anyone who had shared Gruffudd ap Llywelyn's short-lived dream of a strong and united Wales. It seems that from the outset Bleddyn and Rhiwallon were not content to be mere puppets of Harold and the brothers soon turned to the earl's most formidable rival in England, recreating Gruffudd's old alliance with the house of Mercia.

For much of Edward the Confessor's reign the political equilibrium in England had been maintained by keeping a balance between the three great earldoms in the country, Wessex, Mercia and Northumbria.

Edward himself had been brought to the throne from exile in Normandy as something of a compromise candidate and, if the political balance had been maintained, the childless king would have probably been succeeded by another compromise leader in Edgar Ætheling. The catalyst for change and turmoil was the death of Earl Siward of Northumbria in 1055 and the succession to the earldom of Tostig, Harold's brother from the Godwine house of Wessex. Edward's biographer Frank Barlow says that from this point the king abandoned attempts at balancing the three earldoms and instead put his trust in the Godwines, showing particular friendship and favour to Tostig.[1] Ælfgar, then earl of East Anglia and the heir to Mercia, is thought to have held ambitions of his own to rule Northumbria,[2] but instead he found himself exiled at the instigation of the Godwines, which threw him deep into the arms of alliance with Gruffudd ap Llywelyn. In 1055 and again in 1058 Ælfgar was able to use Welsh support to fight his way back from exile and if this formidable Welsh-Mercian axis had survived it seems certain that Harold's path to the kingship of England would have been blocked. But Harold seized on the opportunity presented by Ælfgar's death to launch his assault on Gruffudd's Wales, the loss of Mercian support proving fatal to the Welsh king.

While the possibility that Ælfgar's son and successor Edwin supported the campaign of Harold and Tostig has been noted, it seems more likely that his youth and inexperience – and, perhaps, the shock of his father's death – meant he was incapable of helping Gruffudd; Barlow estimates that he would have been a teenager in 1063.[3] Edwin's elder brother Burgheard, the intended heir of Ælfgar, had died unexpectedly in 1061 when returning from a successful mission to Rome to defend his family's ecclesiastical interests against the power of the Godwines.[4] According to Barlow, Ælfgar's sons had every reason to hate Tostig.[5] The possibility that Edwin was not even allowed to succeed to Mercia immediately has been mooted.[6] There are no royal diplomas extant for 1063–4 to give a definitive answer, but Stephen Baxter believes Edwin did immediately succeed to the earldom and highlights a diploma written at Windsor on 24 May 1065, on which 'Eadwine dux' appears as a witness below the names of Harold and Tostig and their brothers Leofwine and Gyrth.[7]

The 1065 revolt against the Godwines

If this charter suggests that Edwin had been in charge of Mercia since his father's death, it also indicates the weak position in which his family found itself when compared to their traditional rivals, the Godwines. Four Godwine brothers are named on the Windsor diploma, but there is no place for Edwin's younger brother, Morcar. This political situation was the context for the composition of the work entitled the *Life of King Edward* (*Vita Ædwardi Regis*), which was commissioned by Edward's wife, Edith. She was Godwine's daughter – the sister of Harold, Tostig, Leofwine and Gyrth – and the book was designed to laud the success and glory of England when the siblings worked together, as in 1063 and the years that followed:

> These two great brothers [Harold and Tostig] of a cloud-born land,
> The kingdom's sacred oaks, two Hercules,
> Excel all Englishmen when joined in peace;
> And as of yore
> Was held by Atlas here and Hermes there,
> Lest heaven fall and earth sink all around,
> So these angelic Angles with joined strength
> And like agreement guard the English bounds.[8]

However, the events of 1065 and beyond would overtake the writing of the book, turning it into a lament for what the Godwine dynasty would see as the lost opportunities of 1063–5; 'Ah, vicious discord sprung from brother's strife!'[9] Northumbria would prove to be the fault line in the Godwines' power structure, but the first known challenge to the political order they had established in 1063 came in Wales. Harold had rolled back Gruffudd ap Llywelyn's conquests after his Welsh victory, but he seems to have been determined to take this further in Herefordshire and expand his territories westward into lands that the kings of south-east Wales would have considered an important part of their domains. Portskewett, a coastal site on the Severn estuary in southern Gwent, had close connections with the ruling dynasties of south-east Wales in the early middle ages and it seems likely that Caradog ap Gruffudd would have expected to enjoy power there after his support for Harold in 1063. In 1065, however, the *Anglo-Saxon Chronicle* records the following:

In this year before Lammas Earl Harold ordered some building to be done in Wales – at Portskewett – when he had subdued it, and there he got together many goods and thought of having King Edward there for hunting. And when it was all ready, Caradog, son of Gruffudd, went there with all the following he could get and killed nearly all the people who were building there, and they took the goods that were got ready there. We do not know who first suggested this conspiracy. This was done on St Bartholomew's Day [24 August].[10]

The reference to the 'conspiracy' – which is not contained in all versions of the chronicle – is especially intriguing, given the events that would follow. The Tudor historian David Powel has an extended account of the incident, which proposes that Harold had exiled Caradog after 1063 and instead supported Maredudd ab Owain (although it should be noted that Powel's claims to authority are not helped by the fact that he places Harold's argument with Tostig before the events at Portskewett rather than after them):

Caradog ap Gruffudd ap Rhydderch was the first that procured Harold for to come to Wales against Gruffudd ap Llywelyn, hoping by him to attain unto the government of south Wales. But it fell out otherwise, for when Harold understood that he should not get that at the hands of Caradog which he looked for, which was a certain lordship within Wales nigh unto Hereford, and knowing also Caradog to be a subtle and deceitful man, compounding with Maredudd ab Owain for that lordship, he made him king or prince of south Wales, and banished Caradog out of the country. Afterward Harold having obtained that lordship builded there a princely and sumptuous house at a place called Portaslyth [Portskewett], and diverse times earnestly invited the king to come to see the same, and at the length the king being then at Gloucester not far off, granted him his request: whereupon, Harold made such preparation as is before mentioned for him, which was thus most horribly abused by Tostig. Soon after this wicked act, the said Caradog ap Gruffudd came to the same house, and to be revenged upon Harold, killed all the workmen and labourers that were there at work, and all the servants and people of Harold that he could find, and defacing the work, carried away those things that with great labour and expense had been brought thither, to set out and beautify the building.[11]

Caradog's assault on Harold's men may be judged bold, foolish or desperate, but it becomes more understandable if there were wider forces at play offering him support. Such support may have come from Wales and/or Mercia, but there were also other areas that resented the dominance of the Godwines and discontent exploded into the open in Northumbria. There is evidence that Tostig's rule during his ten years in charge of the unruly northern earldom had been harsh – even the *Life of King Edward* describes the 'heavy yoke of his rule'[12] – but it had seemingly been successful as well. It has been suggested that disquiet was caused by his involving Northumbria in the 1063 Welsh campaign; the men of the earldom were not accustomed to troubling themselves with Welsh political affairs, although it may be speculated that this was somehow linked to the poorly evidenced events of 1058, when Gruffudd, Ælfgar and a Norwegian fleet allied for a campaign in England. But the invasion of Wales was successful and yielded booty to the victorious armies, which makes it more likely that the succeeding events of 1063–5 were responsible for the revolt against Tostig. There seem to have been two main factors at play; Tostig's involvement in the bewildering series of blood feuds that characterised relations between the Northumbrian nobility and, more importantly, the increased taxes that he imposed on the region, which led to a rising amongst the lower-class thegns.[13] The *Anglo-Saxon Chronicle* places the revolt immediately after the events at Portskewett although there was over a month between them, Frank Barlow dating the start of the northern rising to 3 October:

> And soon after this [the attack on Portskewett] all the thegns in Yorkshire and Northumberland came together and outlawed their Earl Tostig and killed his bodyguard, and all they could get at, both English and Danish, and took all his weapons in York, and gold and silver and all his treasure they could hear about anywhere. And they sent for Morcar, son of Earl Ælfgar, and chose him as their earl, and he went south with all the people of the shire, and of Nottinghamshire, Derbyshire and Lincolnshire until he came to Northampton. And his brother Edwin came to meet him with the men that were in his earldom, and also many Welsh came with him. Thereupon Earl Harold came to meet them, and they entrusted him with a message to King Edward, and also sent messengers with him, and asked that they might be allowed to have Morcar as their earl. And the king granted this and sent Harold back to them at Northampton on the eve of St Simon and St Jude [28 October]. And he proclaimed this to them and gave them surety for it, and he renewed there the law of King Cnut. And the northern men did much damage round Northampton while he was gone on their errand, in that

they killed people and burned houses and corn and took all the cattle that they could get at which was many thousands – and captured many hundreds of people and took them north with them, so that that shire and other neighbouring shires were the worse for it for many years. And Earl Tostig and his wife and all those who wanted what he wanted went south overseas to Count Baldwin, and he received them all and there they remained all the winter.[14]

The revolt seems to have come as a complete surprise to both the king and Tostig, both of whom – they were apparently close friends – were hunting in Wiltshire at the time;[15] in a rare note of criticism of Tostig, the *Life of King Edward* says that when the storm broke he was 'tarrying down south with the king'.[16] What is clear is that the revolt was directed against Tostig and not the rule of King Edward. Beyond that we need to consider the role of the house of Mercia and the Welsh, plus the part that Harold played in the events. It seems certain both that the rising was coordinated between Northumbria and Mercia and that the alliance between Wales and Mercia had already been re-established. This increases the likelihood that Caradog's attack on Harold at Portskewett was a part of a wider movement against the Godwines, not an isolated incident. The *Anglo-Saxon Chronicle's* reference to a 'conspiracy' at Portskewett has led to speculation that it was part of a growing feud between Harold and Tostig, but this seems unlikely;[17] at this time the brothers were still enjoying the supremacy they had won in 1063 and Portskewett was rather the first open sign of the wider opposition to that hegemony.

The decision of the northern rebels to replace Tostig with Edwin's younger brother Morcar rather than a Northumbrian noble may seem surprising, but there were few local alternatives, and certainly no one who could unite all factions. In 1064 Tostig had arranged the murder of a leading Northumbrian noble called Gospatric, who may have been seen as a suitable earl. It was possibly after Gospatric's death that the local nobility decided to turn to the only family in England capable of offering sufficient support to challenge the power of the Godwines. The *Life of King Edward* describes Edwin and Morcar joining the 'mad conspiracy . . . for there was ill-will from long-standing rivalry between these boys of royal stock and Earl Tostig.[18] As part of the deal that gave Northumbria to Morcar, Osulf of the house of Bamburgh was given control of the far north of the earldom, suggesting that the youthful Morcar was a compromise candidate who was expected to rule in collaboration with the local nobility in a manner that would allow them their traditional rights and tax dues and end the harsh conditions imposed by Tostig.

Having caught the king and Tostig off guard, the rebels were able to make a threatening move south and link their forces with those of Mercia, including the 'many Welsh' accompanying Edwin. The *Life of King Edward* says that the king and the earl found it difficult to gather an effective resistance because 'changing weather was already setting in from hard winter, and it was not easy to raise a sufficient number of troops for a counter offensive'.[19] The rebels marched to Northampton via Lincoln, Nottingham and Derby, before advancing as far as Oxford. This is the appropriate period in which to place Bleddyn's pre-1066 assault on Herefordshire, which was mentioned in Domesday Book; land in Archenfield is recorded as being of unknown value in 1066 because of the attacks that had been made by 'King Gruffudd and Bleddyn in the time of King Edward'. The reference to Gruffudd's attack undoubtedly refers to his great invasion of 1055, while 1065 would seem to be the only possible window of opportunity for Bleddyn to make a similar strike. With the alliance with Mercia back in place and the Godwines struggling to deal with the revolt from their base in Britford near Wilton, Bleddyn revealed the true nature of his ambition as Gruffudd's successor. He targeted the lands of the 'greater Wales' that his half-brother had ruled, lowland territories that formed part of Harold's earldom of Herefordshire. It also seems likely that such an incursion would have been made in alliance with Caradog ap Gruffudd, perhaps indicating that Bleddyn was able to exert some degree of overlordship with regard to the southern Welsh ruler.[20] I would suggest that Caradog's marriage to Bleddyn's daughter, Gwenllian, was arranged around this time. A further indication of cooperation between Caradog and the rulers of Gwynedd-Powys may be found in the reference to a certain 'Ednywain of Gwynedd' who was based in Caradog's territory of Gwynllŵg and was said to be 'a most intimate friend' of his.[21] Gruffudd ap Llywelyn's 1055 assault on Archenfield had come from the south along the Wye, after he had defeated and killed Caradog's father, Gruffudd ap Rhydderch;[22] Bleddyn may have followed the same campaign trail with his son-in-law Caradog, following the latter's successful assault on Portskewett. It is noticeable that when the Normans arrived in Herefordshire they immediately moved to control the invasion route up the Wye valley by building castles at Monmouth and Chepstow.

The context of this attack on Harold's Herefordshire lands needs to be remembered when considering the final piece in the jigsaw of the 1065 revolt, the part played by Harold himself. He came to an accommodation with the rebels that allowed him to succeed Edward on the throne of England and it has been suggested that he may have been a part of the conspiracy from the outset, perhaps as a way to counter the obvious friendship that existed between Tostig and Edward. To support this theory we have the *Anglo-Saxon Chronicle*'s vague references to 'conspiracy', plus the stormy scene described in the *Life of King Edward*.[23] When Edward and the Godwines gathered at Britford, a furious argument ensued during which Harold had to swear an oath that he had played no part in the revolt. Yet despite reporting the rumour – and the work's typically pro-Tostig stance – the *Life of King Edward* does not seem to believe that Harold could have been guilty of the deceit. The fact that the revolt had included an assault on Harold's lands in Herefordshire would also seem to point to that conclusion. Harold was trusted enough to lead the negotiations with the rebels, first at Northampton and then at Oxford. Edward had sent him to the Northampton meeting with the demand that the rebels lay down their arms, after which the king would hear their complaints against Tostig and do them justice. But the rebels' rejection of Tostig was absolute; their response was that if he was not removed they would also make war on Edward. This was followed by their advance to Oxford and Harold's return to Britford with this news would seem the likely context of the argument described in the *Life of King Edward*. The work also makes clear the lack of sympathy for Tostig at court, where the belief that he had brought his problems on himself was widespread. Edward's inability to raise an army left him with no choice but to agree to the rebels' terms and to accept Morcar as Earl of Northumbria. The king was shattered by the refusal of his realm to answer to his will and it is thought that he may have suffered some sort of stroke, leading to incapacity and, eventually, death on 5 January 1066.

The man to profit most from these developments in the short term was, of course, Harold, but this would seem to be thanks to his shrewd handling of the situation rather than his engineering of it. As the events developed he was forced to acknowledge that the Godwines' power play of 1063 had ended and that – if he was to succeed to the throne – he would have to sacrifice his brother and find another way. This meant alliance with his longtime rivals from Mercia. Domesday Book reveals that in 1066 Harold enjoyed significant landholdings in both Mercia and Northumbria, the latter including estates that had formerly been held by Tostig but were then divided between Morcar, Edwin and Harold. Whilst acknowledging that various interpretations can be put on this evidence, Stephen Baxter is of the opinion that it represents redistribution and a compromise agreement after Tostig's exile at the end of 1065.[24] The new détente was sealed by a dynastic marriage, as described by Barlow:

> Before Edward died it must have been agreed that Edwin and Morcar would support Harold's claim to the throne and that Harold would marry their sister, Ealdgyth, Gruffudd ap Llywelyn's widow, and protect them against Tostig. It may also have been at this time that Harold obtained substantial tenements in Mercia, valued in Domesday Book at over £250.[25]

While such a deal is likely to have scuppered any ambitions that Bleddyn and Rhiwallon had to extend their dominion into Harold's Hereford-shire, it also left them considerably stronger than they had been under the heel of the Godwines in 1063. The powerful Welsh-Mercian alliance had been recreated and it seems that the brothers also enjoyed friendly relations with Caradog ap Gruffudd, a position that would have opened the possibility of extending further their dominion over south Wales. But ambitions within Wales were to be put on hold as the brothers found themselves drawn into events that would impact on a much wider, international stage.

1066

Harold's succession to the throne did not, of course, go unchallenged. Duke William of Normandy was soon planning his invasion of England, but the first attacks came from the exiled Tostig. His raids along the east coast were repelled by Edwin and Morcar, but he was able to gather much more significant support from Harold Hardrada, the feared and formidable king of Norway, who had his own claim to the English throne. Tostig and Hardrada began their attack on the north-east in early September with a force of over 300 ships. With Harold Godwinesson on the south coast awaiting the invasion of William, the defence fell to the teenage brothers Edwin and Morcar. We have no direct evidence that there were Welsh troops with the brothers, but given the support that Bleddyn and Rhiwallon had offered in 1065 and their actions in the years after 1066 there would seem to be a strong likelihood of this.[26]

Leaving their ships at Riccall on the Ouse, Hardrada and Tostig began their march on York but found their way blocked by Edwin and Morcar outside the city at Fulford Gate, where battle was joined on 20 September. The nature of the sources for the battle means that little definitive can be said about the clash, but Charles Jones has used his military experience and formidable knowledge of the local topography to attempt a reconstruction which is highly detailed if, inevitably, speculative. He contends that the majority of the Mercian force under Edwin would have been positioned to the west of York to defend the approaches to their homeland.[27] If Bleddyn and Rhiwallon were present, it would seem natural to place them with this force. But it was Morcar's men who, Jones says, met the full force of a diversionary frontal assault ordered by Hardrada, the earl's Northumbrians finding initial success and surging forward as they seemed to gain the upper hand. But, again according to Jones, Hardrada's flanking force was able to bully its way through Edwin's supporting Mercians – only a minority of whom had made it to the battlefield in time – and get in behind Morcar, inflicting great slaughter on the Northumbrians. If we accept Jones's reconstruction, this means that Morcar's force took the greater part of the punishment while Edwin and his men – perhaps including any supporting Welsh force – slipped back to York at the end of the day. Hardrada's success was short-lived; as he tarried over arranging terms with the defeated northerners, Harold Godwinesson's rapid march from the south took the invaders completely by surprise and Hardrada and Tostig were killed in the battle of Stamford Bridge, along with much of their army. There is no evidence that Edwin and Morcar took part in this second battle, but as the English king marched through York on his way to the showdown it is possible that they – and, perhaps, their Welsh allies – joined him.

Even if Edwin and Morcar did join up with Harold for the battle at Stamford Bridge, it does not seem that any significant force from northern England (or Wales) followed the king south to meet the threat of Duke William. The next we hear of the brother earls is after Harold's death at Hastings, when they were amongst the surviving Anglo-Saxon leaders seemingly left paralysed as the duke and his men ravaged the south-east and isolated them in London, prompting submission to William at Barking in January 1067. In March of that year, Edwin, Morcar and other leading Anglo-Saxon nobles were taken to Normandy by William when he made his triumphant return to the duchy, a move that allowed him to keep an eye on them and parade them before his Norman subjects. There is no suggestion that Bleddyn and Rhiwallon were present at Barking, nor that they were taken to Normandy. We can only speculate about what position they felt they were in with regard to the new king of England, particularly as to whether they would continue to pay the dues they had promised to Edward and Harold in 1063; it seems unlikely.

Life under the Norman yoke

The submission of Edwin and Morcar to William had occurred when there were still significant military resources available in Anglo-Saxon England, along with a viable alternative candidate for the kingship in the person of Edgar Ætheling. The shock and fear resulting from the military successes of the Normans would be one explanation for their reluctance to resist, but it also seems likely that they were attempting to play a longer strategic game that they hoped would advance the ambitions of their family. Their sister, Harold's widow Ealdgyth, was pregnant with the ex-king's son (or, possibly, twin sons – the evidence is uncertain) and she had been sent north to the safety of Chester before the brothers submitted to William. Edwin was promised the king's daughter in marriage, giving the family a variety of options that had the potential to keep them at the forefront of English politics for many years to come. That William ever considered this to be a possibility seems unlikely, however, and the indication is that the brothers were treated more like hostages in Normandy and at the king's court than as honourable members of his entourage. Stephen Baxter highlights the fact that their absence is notable from the witness lists of most charters at this time, despite the fact that they would have been at court when the charters were signed.[28]

The position of Edwin and Morcar was closely tied up with the arrangements that William was to make on the Welsh border. Soon after the Norman Conquest three great marcher earldoms were established on the border, Chester, Shrewsbury and Hereford. It is important to consider the timing of their creation, with Hereford being formed before the other two when, within months of Hastings, William's trusted deputy William fitz Osbern was given the earldom formerly held by King Harold. When William headed for Normandy in 1067, England was left in the hands of fitz Osbern and Odo, bishop of Bayeux. As has been noted, fitz Osbern immediately took steps to control the Wye valley invasion route into Herefordshire by building castles at Monmouth and Chepstow, and he was soon encroaching on Mercian lands in Worcestershire.[29] This was an early illustration of Stephen Baxter's point that – in the period 1066–71 – Edwin and Morcar 'lacked influence and credibility at court; lost territory and property to rival earls; were unable to exercise meaningful power within their earldoms; and failed to hold their family's network of patronage and lordship together.'[30]

The harshness of the rule the Normans imposed on their conquered territories was famously described by Orderic Vitalis. He was born near Shrewsbury in 1075, the son of an English mother and a Norman father who was a clerk to Roger of Montgomery, the first earl of Shrewsbury. Orderic spent the first ten years of his life on the Welsh march before moving to the monastery of Saint-Évroul in Normandy where – in the years 1123–41 – he composed his epic work, the *Ecclesiastical History*. Orderic viewed William's action in taking Edwin, Morcar and the other leading English nobles to Normandy in 1067 as 'honourable captivity . . . by this friendly stratagem he ensured that they would cause no disturbances during his absence, and that the people in general, deprived of their leaders, would be powerless to rebel'. He adds that in Normandy they were treated 'virtually as hostages', taken on tour around the duchy and displayed to the incredulous locals.[31] Meanwhile, England suffered, as Orderic described in one of the most famous descriptions of the fall-out from 1066:

> The English were groaning under the Norman yoke, and suffering oppressions from the proud lords who ignored the king's injunctions. The petty lords who were guarding the castles oppressed all the native inhabitants of high and low degree, and heaped shameful burdens on them. For Bishop Odo and William fitz Osbern, the king's viceregents, were so swollen with pride that they would not deign to hear the reasonable plea of the English or give them impartial judgement. When their men-at-arms were guilty of plunder and rape they protected them by force, and wreaked their wrath all the more violently upon those who complained of the cruel wrongs they suffered. And so the English groaned aloud for their lost liberty and plotted ceaselessly to find some way of shaking off a yoke that was so intolerable and unaccustomed.[32]

Resistance to the Normans

The first major rebellion against Norman power occurred in fitz Osbern's Herefordshire and was led by a man known as Eadric the Wild. John of Worcester has the fullest description of events:

> [When the king went to Normandy] he left as guardians of England his brother Odo, bishop of Bayeux, and William fitz Osbern, whom he had made earl in Herefordshire. He ordered that castles be strengthened in various places . . . at that time there lived a powerful thegn Eadric, called Silvaticus, son of Ælfric, brother of Eadric Streona. The Hereford castle garrison as well as Richard, son of Scrob, frequently laid waste his land, which he had refused to hand over to the king, but whenever they attacked him they lost many of their knights and soldiers. Thereupon, about the time of the Assumption [15 August], Eadric calling on the help of the kings of the Welsh, Bleddyn and Rhiwallon, laid waste Herefordshire up to the bridge over the river Lugg, and brought back great spoil.[33]

The *Anglo-Saxon Chronicle* has a shorter account which does not name the Welsh leaders and that is its last mention of Wales and the Welsh until 1081:

> And Eadric Cild and the Welsh became hostile, and fought against the garrison of the castle at Hereford, and inflicted many injuries upon them.[34]

While John of Worcester says that Eadric's lands were attacked because he had refused submission to William, Orderic claims that he had submitted along with Edwin, Morcar and the other English nobles at Barking in early 1067.[35] Whichever version is accepted, it is clear that Eadric's dispute was with his local rival, Richard fitz Scrob. Although he was a Norman, fitz Scrob had not arrived with William in 1066; he was one of the Normans settled in Herefordshire during the reign of Edward the Confessor, when he had founded Richard's Castle. His previous clashes with Welsh forces included defeat at the hands of Gruffudd ap Llywelyn in a battle near Leominster in 1052.[36] This background has led some historians to dismiss Eadric's rising as a localised affair that bore little relation to the national scene, but there are a number of indications that it was much more than that.[37] Eadric was one of the more important noblemen in the service of the house of Mercia, and if fitz Osbern was turning a blind eye to fitz Scrob's mistreatment of Eadric it would seem to be part of the bigger picture as the power of Edwin and Morcar was eroded. It is notable that Bleddyn and Rhiwallon were immediately on hand to resist this assault on their allies, reflecting the strength and importance of the relationship with Mercia and their own continuing interest in Archenfield.

Figure 9. Hereford
Hereford was a key location in the border
wars between England and Wales.

It has been suggested that Caradog ap Gruffudd may have joined Bleddyn and Rhiwallon for their 1065 assault on Herefordshire and it is possible that he was again on hand to support the attack on fitz Scrob. The likelihood of this is supported by evidence which shows that fitz Osbern – who, Orderic says, was placed on the Welsh border to fight the 'bellicose Welsh' – gave land in Herefordshire to Maredudd ab Owain of Deheubarth. In 1086, Domesday Book records seven estates in Herefordshire that were held by Maredudd's son, Gruffudd.[38] The estates were said to have been previously held by Harold, Godric or other Anglo-Saxon nobles and it is stated that William fitz Osbern gave them to 'King Maredudd'; this means that Maredudd did not hold the estates in 1066 and that he must have received them in the period 1067–71. At some point King William also gave his backing to this arrangement, Domesday Book recording that he remitted the geld from the lordship of Lye to King Maredudd and after to his son.[39] As has been seen, Powel believed that Harold Godwinesson had played the power of Maredudd against that of Caradog in the period 1063–5, and the two were natural rivals for the control of south Wales. Bleddyn and Rhiwallon are likely to have believed they had a claim to overlordship over Deheubarth, a view which Maredudd would be unlikely to take in good part.

While the nature of Eadric's revolt was more than local, it was rather less than national. There was also a major rising in south-western England in 1067, centred on Exeter where Harold Godwine's mother Gytha was residing. But, as ever, there was no coordination between the houses of Godwine of Wessex and Leofwine of Mercia, and there was no attempt to link this rising with that of Eadric. Nevertheless, the growing problems helped persuade the king to return from Normandy and he embarked on a winter campaign that forced the submission of Exeter. Included in the king's entourage on his return to England was Roger of Montgomery; he had served as William's loyal regent in Normandy in 1066–7 and was now ready to claim his reward in the form of conquered land.[40] He was immediately given extensive holdings in Sussex, but Roger would also – at an uncertain date – become earl of Shrewsbury, a title that came with wide territorial gains in Shropshire. Such gains would, of course, be at the expense of Mercia, and the creation of new earldoms was part of the process of undermining the powerbase of Edwin and Morcar.

Edwin and Morcar were present at court for the coronation of William's wife Matilda in 1068 and charters reveal that they were both still accorded the title of earl. Soon afterwards they were able to get away from the royal presence and Orderic described what followed:

> The noble youths Edwin and Morcar, sons of Earl Ælfgar, rebelled, and many others with them; so that the realm of Albion was violently disturbed by their fierce insurrection. For when King William had made his peace with Earl Edwin, granting him authority over his brother and almost a third of England, he had promised to give him his daughter in marriage; but later, listening to the dishonest counsels of his envious and greedy Norman followers, he withheld the maiden from the noble youth, who greatly desired her and had long waited for her. At last his patience wore out and he and his brother were roused to rebellion,

supported by a great many of the English and Welsh . . . When the Norman conquest had brought such grievous burdens upon the English, Bleddyn king of the Welsh came to the help of his uncles [*sic*], bringing a great army of Welshmen with him. After large numbers of the leading men of England and Wales had met together, a general outcry arose against the injustice and the tyranny which the Normans and their comrades-in-arms had inflicted on the English. They sent envoys into every corner of Albion to incite men openly and secretly against the enemy. All were ready to conspire together to recover their former liberty, and bind themselves by weighty oaths against the Normans.[41]

In addition to these threats, the Normans had to contend with continued unrest in south-west England, where the sons of Harold were active with the support of troops from Ireland. Edwin and Morcar headed to York, bringing them close to Edgar Ætheling, who had fled to Scotland and found support from King Malcolm, with whom he was planning an invasion. The response from William was typically swift, brutal and effective; he quickly marched north, building castles on the way at Warwick and Nottingham. This show of force was enough to bring a surprisingly swift submission from Edwin and Morcar; in the words of Orderic they were 'unwilling to face the doubtful issue of battle and wisely preferred peace to war'. Perhaps the earls were somewhat battle shy after their mauling at Fulford, or maybe William was able to persuade them that their cooperation would be rewarded. The 'terrified' inhabitants of York soon submitted too and William, having successfully negotiated with Malcolm who called off his invasion, and constructed new castles at York, Lincoln, Huntingdon and Cambridge, was able to return south.

Despite the king's apparent victory, widespread revolt continued in northern and western England for the next two years. Although these risings were in the heartlands of the earls of Mercia and Northumbria, Edwin and Morcar seem to have played no active part and were, most probably, little more than captives at William's court. In the opinion of Marc Morris:

A royal charter, probably drawn up in the spring of 1069, shows they were still at court and being accorded their titles. But to have called Edwin 'earl of Mercia' or Morcar 'earl of Northumbria' must have been tantamount to mockery, for they plainly exercised no real power at all in their respective provinces.[43]

Despite the absence of leadership from the earls, their sworn men, such as Eadric, continued the fight. In reality they probably had little choice; their options were resistance or seeing their powers and privileges appropriated by the Norman invaders. Bleddyn and Rhiwallon remained unwavering in their support of their Mercian associates, showing once again how important they considered this alliance to be to their wider ambitions.

The harrying of Mercia and the north

The resumption of open rebellion began in the far north in early 1069, forcing William to make another expedition to York, where he built a new, stronger castle. Things quietened down until the autumn, when a huge Danish fleet, estimated at 240 ships, landed in the north. It was led by Swein Estrithson, who had a claim to the English throne through his ancestor, Cnut. He joined with Edgar Ætheling and the Anglo-Saxon nobility of Northumbria, their forces combining to defeat the Normans in York. Meanwhile, the revolt of Eadric and his Welsh allies had spread east to Staffordshire and north into Cheshire, as reported by Orderic: 'The Welshmen and men of Chester besieged the royal stronghold at Shrewsbury, and were assisted by the native citizens, the powerful and warlike Eadric the Wild, and other untameable Englishmen.'[44]

Once again William made a swift and effective march north to York, and once again the reluctance of his enemies to engage him in force brought the king relief, as the Danes and Anglo-Saxons pulled back from the city. This allowed William to leave a holding force to contain the Danes in the north before setting out from Lindsey to Shrewsbury, where he quickly defeated the Anglo-Welsh force besieging the castle. William marched back north, beginning his infamous ravaging of the country, which would break the will of the resistance and leave large swathes of England facing misery for years to come, as revealed by the evidence of Domesday Book seventeen years later. Frank Stenton called the campaign 'the most terrible visitation that had ever fallen on any large part of England since the Danish wars of Alfred's time', while John Gillingham says that it was this military action, not the battle of Hastings, that secured the conquest, demonstrating as it did 'the supreme example of the soldier's brutal art'.[45] The king bought off the Danes in York before continuing the harrying of the countryside that prompted the submission of the leading Anglo-Saxon rebels in the north, Waltheof and Cospatric. Even then the intensity of William's campaign did not slacken and, in the depths of winter, he led his army over the Pennines towards Chester. Orderic reports that women in Normandy were telling their husbands to leave the dangers of England and come home, while the king's 'loyal barons and stalwart fighting men were gravely perturbed' by continual risings; the winter march was very nearly the final straw as the troops came close to rebelling.[46] But William's generalship held the army together and the shock of his appearance in the Cheshire plain quickly forced the capitulation of the remaining Mercian and Welsh resistance. After building castles at Chester and Stafford the king was free to return south. While at Salisbury shortly before Easter 1070 he was confident enough to disband the mercenary element of his army and Brian Golding claims that 'the Easter court of 1070 in many respects marks the conclusion of the military stage of conquest [of England]'.[47]

The battle of Mechain

While the sources make clear the Welsh support for the Mercian rising, the ability of Bleddyn and Rhiwallon to lend the full weight of their power would have been limited by problems within Wales that may well have been fuelled by Norman interference. The various versions of the Welsh chronicle for the year 1069 are concerned only with an epochal battle and its fall-out:

> And then was the battle of Mechain between Bleddyn and Rhiwallon, sons of Cynfyn, and Maredudd and [Idwal], sons of Gruffudd. And then the sons of Gruffudd fell: [Idwal] was slain in the battle, and Maredudd died of cold in flight. And there Rhiwallon ap Cynfyn was slain. And then Bleddyn ap Cynfyn held Gwynedd and Powys, and Maredudd ab Owain ab Edwin held Deheubarth.[48]

The opposing forces joined battle in Mechain. We cannot locate the battle site more precisely, but according to tradition it was at Llanfechain, which seems to have been in the heartlands of the power-base of the family of Cynfyn and which I have suggested may have served as something of a 'capital' for the dynasty. If this was the case, perhaps the winter date might suggest that Maredudd and Idwal tried to copy the tactic used by Harold in December 1062, when he surprised Gruffudd ap Llywelyn at his midwinter court in Rhuddlan.[49] A local tradition says that the battle was fought near St Garmon's Well and that, after it, the sons of Gruffudd were buried under a mound in a nearby field.[50] It has been noted that Gruffudd ap Llywelyn's eldest son is thought to have been the Owain ap Gruffudd who died in 1059. Maredudd seems to have been the king's next eldest son and the man being groomed as his successor; he is named twice in charters in the Book of Llandaff as being present at events dated to the period 1056–63, where he is the second most prominent layman, preceded only by Gruffudd himself. Idwal is otherwise unknown, his obscurity highlighted by the fact that Welsh chroniclers were unsure of his name; the *Brutiau* have 'Ithel', but the *Annales Cambriae* texts have Idwal.[51] Both Maredudd and Idwal may have been minors at the time of their father's death in 1063; certainly they seem to have been in no position to be major players in Wales in the immediate aftermath of Harold's victorious campaign. It is possible that they remained in Wales under the close watch of their father's half-brothers, Bleddyn and Rhiwallon. However, the *Life of King Edward* says that, at the end of their 1063 campaign, Harold and Tostig gave King Edward 'looted treasures and the hostages as proof of victory'.[52] The sons of the defeated Welsh king are prime candidates to have been such hostages. If this was their fate, they may have fallen into Norman hands after 1066; with Bleddyn and Rhiwallon so steadfast in support of William's enemies, the sons of the former king of Wales may have had little trouble in winning Norman military backing for an attempt to restore their family's fortunes. The uncertain dates associated with our source material make any close association with William's campaigns no more than speculative, but the death of Maredudd 'by cold in flight' points to a winter battle and makes it tempting to suggest that there was some coordination between this clash and William's winter march on Chester in 1069. More localised Norman support would also seem a very realistic possibility, given the recent hostility in Herefordshire between Richard fitz Scrob and Bleddyn, Rhiwallon and Eadric.

The attitude of the Welsh chronicle may also suggest that the sons of Gruffudd had enjoyed significant support in Wales, although this was perhaps more on a moral than a practical, military level. The chronicle entries for 1069 are the first mention of Bleddyn and the only time they name Rhiwallon directly. The reference to Bleddyn's rule after the battle could suggest that the chroniclers did not consider his succession to Gruffudd ap Llywelyn as clear before this point, perhaps an indication of support for the sons of Gruffudd as the rightful rulers of Wales. The statement that Maredudd ab Owain ruled Deheubarth after the battle of Mechain could be a further indication of this support, as well as a suggestion that Maredudd had taken advantage of the distraction of his Welsh rivals to consolidate his power in the south. In the years to come Maredudd would certainly threaten Caradog ap Gruffudd in south-east Wales and Brycheiniog, and we may speculate that he also contended for power in Ceredigion.

Battles were unusual events at that time, as military power was traditionally imposed by the ravaging of an opponent's territory. Leaders would generally avoid direct confrontations because of the dangers they posed to all involved, their uncertainty and the fact that they were frequently not decisive. As the Roman writer Vegetius, whose military manuals were well known, respected and used throughout medieval Europe, wrote:

> It is much better to overcome the enemy by famine, surprise or terror than by general action, for in the latter instance fortune has often a greater share than valour . . . Good officers never engage in general actions unless induced by opportunity or obliged by necessity.[53]

Before Mechain, the last known battle between named rival Welsh leaders had been in 1044, Gruffudd ap Llywelyn's dominance in his later years proving enough to deter any such direct challenges. Despite Bleddyn's active military life, Mechain is the only battle he is known to have engaged in, although the possibility that he fought at Fulford has been mooted. The clash was most probably forced by his enemies, the sons of Gruffudd, who had everything to gain from a successful encounter; with Bleddyn distracted by the wider strategic picture and the possibility that the sons of Gruffudd enjoyed temporary Norman support, this may have been the only window of opportunity for Maredudd and Idwal to win themselves a position of power in Wales.

The bloody demise of his brother Rhiwallon and his nephews in the battle would only have emphasised to Bleddyn the dangers and uncertainties presented by such an engagement. Mechain, however, was the first in a bitter series of inter-Welsh battles that would dominate the political scene in the country in the decades to come. The chaos that ensued in the fall-out from these wasteful clashes merely emphasised that battles were not the most effective way to settle political disputes. Furthermore, the disruption of Welsh native rule helped clear the way for Norman interference, conquest and colonisation of the country. This was not immediately clear in 1069; Bleddyn walked away from the battlefield having lost his ally and brother, but as undisputed king of Gwynedd-Powys and having removed two dynastic rivals who had a compelling claim to his crown. However, this has to be set in the context of the wider political scene; it was clear that the Mercian alliance that had been such a central pillar in his power structure was no longer of any relevance, while the challenges Bleddyn faced from south Wales had also increased.

5

Opportunity and Disaster

If the breaking of the power of Bleddyn's allies Edwin and Morcar had intially been a painfully protracted affair, it proceeded at some speed after William's brutal 1069–70 winter campaign. Although the 1068–70 risings against the king had largely been conducted on the lands of the brother earls, neither Edwin nor Morcar were named amongst the opposition, probably indicating that they were virtual captives at William's court. In his assessment of the history of the great Mercian dynasty in the tenth and eleventh centuries, Stephen Baxter says:

> The Leofwinesons held onto comital power for longer than any of their peers. They did so by augmenting and protecting the powers vested in them as agents of royal government, principally by constructing local networks of land, patronage and lordship; but these networks were subject to extraordinary pressures between 1066 and 1071, and eventually collapsed; and the moment they did so, the house of Leofwine fell.[1]

Furthermore:

> Between 1066 and 1071, Edwin and Morcar lacked influence at the Conqueror's court; their alliances with the Welsh and the house of Bamburgh were smashed; they gradually lost their ability to exercise meaningful power within the shires and towns within their earldoms; they were forced to cede territory and property to the Conqueror's followers; their family's network of monastic clients fell apart; and they proved unable to provide good lordship to their men.[2]

Above all, William's infamous harrying of the north had proved to the earls' retained men that Edwin and Morcar could not fulfil the most crucial role of a lord, to defend those in their service. Baxter highlights the fact that 'Domesday Book proves that virtually all of the estates held by the Leofwinesons' commended men in 1066 were controlled by other lords in 1086.'[3] The great rebel Eadric the Wild submitted to William and was reconciled to him in 1070 and it seems reasonable to assume that Bleddyn, who had been so closely associated with Eadric's campaigns, ended his open conflict with the king at the same time.

After this the fate of Edwin and Morcar forms little more than a footnote to Bleddyn's story. The unfortunate brothers would have gained some hope from the arrival of Swein Estrithson in England in 1070, as he joined the Danish fleet in the Humber that William had previously bought off. This encouraged more English revolts in Lincolnshire which were made famous by another of the Leofwinesons' commended men, Hereward the Wake. William made peace with the Danes in the summer and they left England, but Hereward fought on from the Isle of Ely and, during the winter, Edwin and Morcar were able to slip away from the king's court and attempt to join the rebels. It was, however, too late for any leadership from them to be effective, and the *Anglo-Saxon Chronicle* has the following dismissive account: 'Earl Edwin and Earl Morcar fled away and travelled aimlessly in woods and moors. Then Earl Morcar went to Ely in a ship, and Earl Edwin was killed treacherously by his own men.'[4] Orderic Vitalis has a much more elaborate and favourable account of the actions of the earls and suggests that, even at this late stage, Edwin was attempting to reach out to his old Welsh allies; Orderic claims that the earl spent six months trying to rally support from the Scots, Welsh and English.[5] The lack of response he received would tie in with the suggestion that Eadric and Bleddyn had both made their peace with William in 1070. Edwin's position appears to have been hopeless and he was on his way to Scotland to try to gain help when he was betrayed and killed by his own men; it is an incident that bears comparison with the fate of Gruffudd ap Llywelyn in 1063. Morcar was able to join up with the other rebels on the Isle of Ely, but when this stronghold fell in the summer of 1071 he was captured and was to remain a prisoner for the rest of his life. William followed up his successes with an expedition to Scotland in the summer of 1072 which brought King Malcolm to heel, snuffing out the danger of any more interference from that source.

The earldoms on the Welsh march

The erosion of Edwin and Morcar's 'local networks of land, patronage and lordship' has been considered, but the transfer of their powers into Norman hands was most obviously seen with the creation of new earldoms within their territory, including the three in Mercia's traditional spheres of interest on the Welsh border. According to Marc Morris:

> As early as 1068 Edwin's authority had been seriously compromised by the establishment of rival earldoms centred on Hereford and Shrewsbury for William fitz Osbern and Roger of Montgomery; since the start of 1070 it had been dealt a further and probably fatal blow with the creation of another new earldom based on Chester and given to Gherbod, one of the Conqueror's Flemish followers.[6]

The timescale for the creation of each earldom may not be quite as conclusive as this passage indicates; Orderic suggests that it was only after the final defeat of Edwin and Morcar that William divided up England between his followers.[7] But Stephen Baxter believes that 'King William installed at least one and probably three new earls to commands along the Welsh border while Edwin remained in power.'[8] He says that this was partly for defence and partly to end the dangerous and long-running Welsh-Mercian alliance. These new earldoms had been established on hostile English territory and it would take some time for them to prove a threat to Bleddyn and the other Welsh leaders. But the fact that they had been created in such a hostile environment meant that they were geared for war, and as they settled they would prove a formidable presence on the Welsh scene. Each of the three earls was granted the royal demesne in their county as well as control of the county town, while many of the other landholders in the earl-dom were tenants-in-chief of the earl directly, rather than of the king. The marcher earls in Chester and Shrewsbury treated their leading men in a similar manner to the way the king had treated them; they recognised the military demands of the borderlands and so rearranged Anglo-Saxon estates in order to give their men compact, powerful blocks of land which afforded them significant scope for independent action.[9]

For the previous twenty to thirty years, most of Wales's vulnerable eastern border had been protected by the bulwark of a friendly Mercia;

only in the southern borderlands was there continual conflict with the rulers of Herefordshire. But now Bleddyn and the other Welsh leaders would have to deal with new challenges along the full length of Wales's eastern border. From the early years, the marcher earls involved themselves in Welsh politics, while Bleddyn and the other Welsh leaders dealt with each of them on an individual basis, allowing for both alliance and hostility. We shall consider each earldom in turn, moving from north to south.

The earldom of Chester

William's campaign of 1069–70 into the Cheshire plain is the obvious event to associate with the creation of the earldom of Chester. The fact that it took its name from the great Mercian city and port would have clearly indicated that Edwin's own earldom was soon to be at an end. The new earl, Gherbod, did not find the new land to his taste because, according to Orderic, 'he was continually molested by the English and the Welsh alike'.[10] He soon returned to his continental home and the earldom passed to Hugh of Avranches. Orderic was critical of the new earl's appetites and excesses, saying that he, 'with Robert of Rhuddlan, Robert of Malpas, and other fierce knights, wrought great slaughter amongst the Welsh. He was more prodigal than generous; and went about surrounded by an army instead of a household.'[11]

After the years of revolt and William's ravaging, some serious consolidation would have been required in the earldom, as highlighted by Domesday Book's description of Chester itself: 'When Earl Hugh acquired it, its value was only £30, for it was thoroughly devastated; there were 205 houses less than before 1066. Now there are as many as he found there.'[12] But, despite the devastation throughout his newly acquired earldom, Hugh soon seems to have been able to secure his hold on the manors of Coleshill, Hawarden and Bistre; although these were under Welsh control in the reign of Gruffudd ap Llywelyn, they were held by Edwin in 1063 and Bleddyn does not seem ever to have ruled there. Hugh delegated control of this area and, eventually, responsibility for any future advance against the Welsh to his cousin, Robert of Rhuddlan. Rees Davies memorably described Robert as 'the exemplar of the swashbuckling Norman warrior: endless in his ambition, pride, and greed, combining the most ruthless butchery with the most conventional piety, insatiable in his lust for adventure and battle.'[13] Robert soon constructed a castle on the site of Gruffudd's court at Twthill, Rhuddlan, and he would be a formidable and feared presence on the Welsh political scene for the next twenty years. He is also one of the best-documented of the Norman invaders, largely thanks to vivid descriptions of his activities by Orderic Vitalis, which emphasise how he advanced deep into Gwynedd, building more castles and mercilessly slaughtering his enemies.[14] Such conquests are, however, best understood as occurring after the death of Bleddyn, who seems to have kept Robert in check and may even have threatened his position in north-east Wales. The only direct reference to a clash involving the two men is contained in Orderic's elegy for Robert, which glories in the many victories he won against the Welsh:

With a few men he [Robert] ambushed great [*sic*] king Bleddyn
And made him fly abandoning rich booty.[15]

This reference has been used as evidence of the pressure that Robert was exerting on Wales, but it seems clear that Bleddyn was the one on the attack. I would place these events in the period 1071–3, before the Welsh king was distracted by happenings in the south-west. The fact that Bleddyn had to 'abandon rich booty' would suggest that he was engaged in a ravaging raid against Robert's land, perhaps even attempting to reclaim some of the territory that had been ruled by Gruffudd. On this occasion he was undone by Robert's military skill, the Norman using the element of surprise to strike at an enemy who was slowed down by the spoils of war. Despite Bleddyn's defeat, Orderic's use of the title king seems significant, highlighting the respect granted to the Welshman's power and status; Robert's victory over such a foe redounds to his credit. There is nothing to suggest that Robert made any significant headway into Bleddyn's territory during the latter's lifetime, although it is possible that Bleddyn's attack may have created an enmity between the two.

The earldom of Shrewsbury

As has been seen, the new earl of Shrewsbury, Roger of Montgomery, came to England in 1067 to claim the reward for his successful stint as regent of Normandy in William's absence. His first significant land

77

grants were in Sussex in 1067–8 and it is possible that he started to accrue land in Shropshire at much the same time, although John Mason believes that this only happened after the fall of Edwin in 1070–1.[16] His holdings certainly increased after Edwin's demise, the king granting Roger all of Shropshire save for between fifty and sixty manors on the southern fringes of the shire where, Mason notes, followers of William fitz Osbern in Herefordshire 'had apparently already intruded themselves.[17] Roger saw the value of holding a concentrated block of land and granted the same advantage to his tenants-in-chief when he divided up the shire into three main sections, each of which covered their own stretches of the Welsh border:

> The flatter country north of the Severn and round Oswestry went to his niece's husband Warin, the broken country south of the river round Caus and Longden to Corbet, and the Clun and Onny valleys to Picot (Robert) de Say.[18]

Warin 'the Bald' was the earldom's first sheriff and, as described by Orderic, he played the key role in subduing the English and Welsh opposition in the territory, being employed by Roger 'to crush the Welsh and other opponents and pacify the whole province placed under his rule'.[19] He was given more than seventy manors in Shropshire along with other estates in Warwickshire, Staffordshire and Sussex, making him a power in Shropshire second only to the earl himself. The extent of the challenge facing him is seen in Domesday Book, which described eleven manors in Mersete Hundred as being waste when Warin came to office, but recorded that five (Whittington, Weston, Maesbury, Moreton and Wykey) had been rehabilitated by 1086; Frederick Suppe concluded that by the time of Warin's death in 1085 he had 'brought relative peace to the country'.[20]

From the outset the Normans in Shropshire seem to have had the ambition to explore the boundaries of the earldom to the west, starting by securing land beyond Offa's Dyke that had been held by Mercia but won back by the Welsh in the eleventh century. The place that would become known as Montgomery – named after Roger's homeland in the Pays d'Auge region of Normandy – was a key strategic spot and the invaders focused on a site named Hen Domen, located over a mile to the north-west of the modern town. Hen Domen overlooks the important ford of the Severn to the west known as Rhydwhyman and the plain to the east that includes the area where the battle of Rhyd-y-groes was fought in 1039. This was a famous victory won by Gruffudd ap Llywelyn over the Mercians at the very outset of his reign, a triumph that left him in control of this region of the border and prepared the way for the expansion into lands east of Offa's Dyke that characterised the great king's reign.[21] Indeed, the region seems to have been disputed between the Welsh and the Anglo-Saxons for much of the first half of the eleventh century. The area around Hen Domen was settled with nucleated villages and hamlets with Saxon names, but Domesday Book records that, at the end of the reign of Edward the Confessor, twenty-two of the surrounding vills with 521 hides of arable land were 'waste', a categorisation that is typically seen as the result of Welsh aggression and/or rule. This land had returned to Anglo-Saxon control after 1063 and had been granted to three thegns – Sewar, Oslac and Azor – who were using the region as a hunting ground.[22] The thegns held a further nine manors which were recorded as waste in 1066 but had been in recent cultivation. Included amongst these were Horseforde and Staurecote, which were adjacent to the site of Hen Domen where the Normans built a classic motte and bailey castle, a fortification that has been the subject of many years of archaeological investigation and study.[23]

It is possible that the castle was built on top of an existing Welsh court of Gruffudd's, a practice that the Normans were to follow at Rhuddlan and various other Welsh sites. The fortification was constructed at some point in the 1070s and the strategic site remained in use even after the stone castle of Montgomery was built in 1223. While it is difficult to determine the timescale of construction and development Hen Domen seems from its early days to have been a heavily defended site, with double ramparts and ditches, and archaeological evidence shows the overwhelmingly military character of the occupation. During its construction an adjacent arable field was destroyed, suggesting the importance given to military over economic needs, even in such a devastated piece of territory. The danger posed by the Welsh and their interest in the site was shown in 1095, when the garrison of the castle was massacred during a Welsh revolt led by Bleddyn's son, Cadwgan. The rebuilt twelfth-century castle that has been investigated by archaeologists was formidably defended, with concentric fortifications of 'quite massive proportions, reinforced by deep ditches in places mud – if not water – filled . . . [it is estimated] that the distance from the bottom of the inner ditches to the top of the bailey was some 10 m (33 ft).'[24] Philip Barker and Robert Higham add that any attackers who made it inside the bailey would face vicious street fighting and the necessity of taking each building individually; they would be surrounded on all sides and under the shadow of the tower on top of the motte. It is hard to imagine anything on this sort of scale being constructed during the reign of Bleddyn, but the presence of even the most modest fortification on such a sensitive site could be seen as a source of discomfort and embarrassment to the Welsh king and an encroachment of Norman power. However, it is important to note that Bleddyn had never ruled this territory and – as discussed below – I favour an alternative explanation, which may have seen Bleddyn making an alliance with his new neighbours to further his ambitions in south-west Wales. By accepting the Normans' claim to Hen Domen and the lowlands below it, he was acknowledging that such territory on his eastern border was beyond the reach of his rule and that his ambitions should turn west to territory behind Wales's mountain barriers.

If such a strategy was feasible under a powerful Welsh leader like Bleddyn, it set a dangerous precedent that would cause problems for his weaker successors. Hen Domen would be used as a base for future expansion up the Severn valley, with a number of mottes being built as bases from which the Normans could extend influence and control over neighbouring Welsh regions; examples include Bryn Derwen, Newtown Gro Trump and Rhos Diarbed (Moat Farm). To control and extend the border, the invaders organised their castles for mutual support, helped in the Oswestry region by the employment of light horsemen known as *muntatores*. The full realisation of such organisation was, however, far from complete in the early 1070s. When Warin died in 1085 he was succeeded as sheriff by Rainald de Bailleul-en-Gouffern and Domesday Book evidence shows the early beginnings of muntatorial tenure under him; when Rainald became sheriff, future muntatorial manors such as Brockton were waste and paying no rent, but by 1086 they were 'at least partially rehabilitated and paying rent'.[25] Suppe suggested that, at a similar time, Rainald was building the castle of Oswestry and planning its defence by enfeoffing subvassals under terms of muntatorial tenure. Other castles such as Clun, which would strengthen the Norman grip on the territory and bolster the security of key sites like Hen Domen, were not yet in existence; Suppe suggests that Clun was part of a more systematic plan for border defence ordered by William Rufus after the great Welsh revolt of 1094–5.[26] In the 1070s the Normans in Shropshire would have still

felt very aware of, and vulnerable to, Welsh power. A mutually bene-
ficial alliance that built on the relationships that had existed between
the Welsh and the rulers of Mercia would have been an attractive
proposition.

The earldom of Hereford

The comments of Orderic Vitalis tend rather to confuse the events
of the early years of the earldom of Hereford. He wrote that it was
only after the defeat of Edwin and Morcar in 1070–1 that King
William divided up the lands of England, with William fitz Osbern
and other trusted deputies put into the march to 'fight the bellicose
Welsh'.[27] However, it has been seen that Hereford, the first of the
great marcher earldoms established on the Welsh border, was created
and given to fitz Osbern within months of the victory at Hastings,
and it seems to have been organised in a different manner from the
other two. Fitz Osbern did not receive the entire county in fief, as
happened in Chester and Shrewsbury, and except in certain cases
close to the border, the earl did not typically enfeoff his tenants-
in-chief with compact blocks of estates; Domesday Book reveals
that the estates of one Englishman tended to be granted to one
Frenchman.[28]

Orderic follows his line about the establishment of the marcher
earldoms by stating: 'Since his followers would dare anything, fitz
Osbern made a first attack on Brecknock, and defeated the Welsh
kings Rhys, Cadwgan, Maredudd, and many others.' However, it needs
to be made clear that this attack is highly unlikely to have occurred
soon after the creation of the earldom; in the period 1067–70 the
Normans in Herefordshire were on the defensive against the Welsh,
the early construction of the castles of Chepstow and Monmouth
being a response to the major raids up the Wye valley that had occurred in 1055 and, most probably, 1065 and 1067. The widespread
risings throughout England in 1067–70 would also have limited fitz
Osbern's ability to conduct such an aggressive expedition into Welsh
territory. The campaign must, though, have occurred before 1071,
when fitz Osbern was drawn back to the continent; he met his demise
at the battle of Cassel on 22 February 1071. It could be argued that
the expedition into Brycheiniog was intended to undermine and
distract the Mercians' Welsh allies at the height of the Anglo-Saxon

revolt in 1069, potentially linking it with any Norman support for the forces opposing Bleddyn and Rhiwallon at the battle of Mechain. However, Orderic places the events after the creation of the earldom of Chester in 1070 and such a date would seem logical, the effective end of Anglo-Saxon resistance in Mercia allowing the Normans of Herefordshire to take the offensive.

Another reason to place the event in 1070 is that the three kings whom Orderic says were attacked by fitz Osbern in Brycheiniog – Maredudd, Cadwgan and Rhys – are not the men we would expect to be ruling in that part of Wales before that year.[29] The identification of the first two kings seems reasonably secure, Maredudd being Maredudd ab Owain of Deheubarth, and Cadwgan being Cadwgan ap Meurig, of the traditional royal line of Glamorgan. John Edward Lloyd identified Rhys as being Cadwgan's brother, Rhys ap Meurig;[30] this is certainly a possibility, although I feel it is more likely to have been Maredudd's brother, Rhys ab Owain. In either case, the king named as Rhys is likely to have been a subordinate of his brother. To have these three kings active in Brycheiniog does not accord with the evidence from the Book of Llandaff that gives a picture of the political scene in south-east Wales that prevailed c. 1067.[31] This has Caradog ap Gruffudd ruling in Gwynllŵg, Upper Gwent and Ystrad Yw, the latter region defined by David Crouch as 'the area of Brycheiniog approximating to the cantref of Talgarth' and including much of the Usk valley from its mouth to Tretower. This has been suggested as another indication of the strength of the alliance between Caradog and Bleddyn; the northern ruler's predecessor, Gruffudd ap Llywelyn, had spent years campaigning in the Talgarth area, where he won some of his greatest victories over the Anglo-Saxons, but Bleddyn seems content to have allowed his son-in-law Caradog to enjoy rule in the region. Meanwhile, according to the Book of Llandaff, Caradog's cousin, Rhydderch ap Caradog, was ruling Lower Gwent and Ewias c. 1067, while Glamorgan was held by Cadwgan ap Meurig.

William fitz Osbern's actions cannot be seen in a simple 'Normans v. Welsh' context. The time taken for the Normans to begin their penetration of Gwent and lowland south-east Wales has often been remarked upon and explained by their friendly relations with Caradog ap Gruffudd.[32] As has been seen, Caradog was Bleddyn's son-in-law and our evidence suggests that the two acted in concert on a number of occasions. There is also a suggestion that Bleddyn's cessation of hostility with the Normans in 1070 may have been accompanied by a peace deal with his former enemies from Herefordshire. The key to this may have been Bleddyn's niece, Nest, the daughter of Gruffudd ap Llywelyn and Ealdgyth. Nest must have been born in the period 1056–64 and was presumably with her twice-widowed mother when Ealdgyth was sent to Chester in the aftermath of Hastings. What happened to mother and daughter when the Normans overran Chester in 1070 is unknown, but the chief champions of Ealdgyth's brothers Edwin and Morcar in the west had been Bleddyn and Eadric. For the noble ladies to have sought protection from a relative across the Welsh border would have been a logical course of action and this suggestion is possibly strengthened by the *Brutiau*'s description of Bleddyn as a 'defender of orphans and of the weak and of widows'. We know that Nest was at some point married to Osbern fitz Richard, the son of Richard fitz Scrob, the enemy of Eadric and Bleddyn, who, it has been suggested, may have been involved in the alliance against the latter before the battle of Mechain. The year 1070 would seem a logical date to have arranged this marriage as part of a peace treaty that saw Bleddyn and Eadric end their open hostility to Norman rule. If Nest was born soon after her mother's marriage to Gruffudd she would have reached marriageable age by 1070 and this timescale would also fit with the dates and activities we can trace for her daughter with Osbern, Agnes, and Agnes's daughter, Sibyl.[33] Nest would have been an attractive wife for Osbern, thanks both to her noble bloodline and her wealth. Domesday Book records that in 1086 Osbern was holding land in Warwickshire that had formerly been held by Ealdgyth and had, presumably, come to him through Nest.[34] In later years Coventry Abbey, which was founded by Ealdgyth's grandfather Leofric, was to buy the lands of Eaton-in-Dee from Osbern, an estate which is again thought to have come to him through his marriage.[35]

Another part of any peace deal arranged by Bleddyn and Caradog with the Normans of Herefordshire is likely to have seen their rival Maredudd stripped of the lands he held in the county; these lands had been granted to him by William fitz Osbern, but later needed to be re-granted to Maredudd's son Gruffudd by William the Conqueror, perhaps suggesting that they had been lost to the family for a time. The loss of the Herefordshire lands would have been made easier by Maredudd's concentration on Deheubarth, where the various versions of the Welsh chronicle claim that he started to rule in 1069, after the battle of Mechain. This may also have been the time when Maredudd began to increase his pressure on south-east Wales, gathering his forces from the south-west and allying with Cadwgan ap Meurig for an attack on Caradog ap Gruffudd in Brycheiniog. This would seem to be the context for Orderic's account of William fitz Osbern's defeat of Maredudd, Cadwgan and Rhys and it is likely that Caradog and his supporters fought alongside their Norman allies.[36]

The challenge from Deheubarth

We hear no more of Cadwgan ap Meurig, nor of his brother Rhys, the last in the direct line of kings of Glamorgan, which can be traced back to Hywel ap Rhys in the ninth century. It is possible that they were killed or driven off in the clash with fitz Osbern or, perhaps, in the related battle of Rhymney in 1072, which again saw Caradog ally with the Normans. According to *Brut (RBH)*: 'Maredudd ab Owain was slain by Caradog ap Gruffudd ap Rhydderch and the French on the banks of the river Rhymney.' The Rhymney marks the traditional boundary between Glamorgan and Gwent; although we cannot locate the battle more precisely, I would suggest that the most likely spot would be in the lowlands close to the river's confluence with the sea. A battlefield close to the site of Rumney Castle (thought to have been constructed *c.* 1081) is a possibility; the fortification would guard the river crossing and was regarded as the western boundary of the later marcher lordship of Gwynllŵg. The fact that Maredudd was campaigning so far to the east of his heartland in Deheubarth would seem to indicate that he was the aggressor – perhaps threatening a *maerdref* of Caradog's in the region of modern- day Newport – and that his setback at the hands of fitz Osbern in Brycheiniog had not severely restricted his power. The lack of a mention for either of the sons of Meurig could even suggest that Maredudd was ruling directly in Glamorgan; however, the various versions of the Welsh chronicle make no mention of Cadwgan or Rhys ap Meurig in any of their entries, meaning that it is dangerous to read too much into the brothers' absence from the 1072 record. Whatever the situation before the battle, the death of Maredudd and Caradog's victory left the latter as the dominant ruler in south-east Wales. Serious opposition remained in Deheubarth in the form of Maredudd's brother, Rhys ab Owain, but momentum had shifted and for the next few years the scenes of the conflict would be in the south-west of Wales, not the south-east.

This major reversal for the ruling dynasty of Deheubarth would have presented an opportunity for Bleddyn. It has been suggested that events around the time of the battle of Mechain had allowed Maredudd to challenge Gwynedd-Powys for control of Ceredigion, which was traditionally disputed territory between the northern kingdom and Deheubarth. The chronicle says that Maredudd ruled Deheubarth from 1069; it never says that Bleddyn held Deheubarth, although the description of him in the *Brutiau* after his death as 'King of the Britons' would imply such authority. This was presumably in the period 1072–5; it was only after the death of Bleddyn in 1075 that Rhys ab Owain and Rhydderch ap Caradog were said to have held Deheubarth. The belief that Bleddyn seized on the opportunity presented by the death of Maredudd to reclaim lost territory in Ceredigion and advance even deeper into south-west Wales can only be inferred, but other evidence can be used to support such a conclusion.

Figure 10. St Davids
Control of St Davids was vital to any ruler wishing
to claim leadership in Deheubarth.

The career of the renowned churchman and scholar Sulien is one such piece of evidence. As has been noted, he was head of the religious community (W. *clas*) at Llanbadarn Fawr in northern Ceredigion and his family had a major hand in the writing and development of the

Brutiau, which show such notable bias in favour of Bleddyn and his family. In 1073 Sulien moved from Ceredigion to Dyfed to become bishop of St Davids, the first of two separate periods in the office (1073–78 and 1079/80–1085/6). It is, of course, entirely possible that Sulien's religious and scholarly reputation was enough to win him control of Dyfed's most famous church. The moral force exerted by St Davids and the propaganda that it could disseminate would, however, be crucial to any ruler hoping to control Deheubarth and it is tempting to see Bleddyn's influence behind Sulien's first appointment.[37] Maredudd's death in 1072 would have left Deheubarth vulnerable and it is possible that Bleddyn used the opportunity to advance into Dyfed and take control of St Davids.

What the inter-Welsh political rivalry in Deheubarth undoubtedly did was open up the country to further alien interference. This is clear from consecutive entries in the *Brutiau*, starting with 1073:

> And then the French ravaged Ceredigion and Dyfed. And Menevia and Bangor were ravaged by the Gentiles. And then died Bleiddudd, bishop of Menevia; and Sulien assumed the bishopric.[38]

The entry for 1074 reads:

> Then for the second time the French ravaged Ceredigion.[39]

If the overall picture of the increasing influence of outside forces is clear, the lack of detail is frustrating and open to any number of interpretations. To deal with the 'French' first; we know from *Annales Cambriae* that the 1074 attack was made by Normans from the earldom of Shrewsbury led by Earl Roger's son Hugh, perhaps pushing forward from their new base at Hen Domen. It seems most likely that they were also responsible for the 1073 attack, but we cannot rule out the possibility that the earlier strike was made by Caradog's allies from Herefordshire, or by a combination of 'French' forces. Meanwhile, the attack from the 'Gentiles' is the first mention in the Welsh chronicles of such a raid since the foundering of a fleet from Ireland that was heading to Deheubarth in 1052.

One thing that may be inferred from future events is that Bleddyn was on the front foot following the campaigns of 1073 and 1074. My favoured interpretation of the evidence – it can be put no stronger than that – would be to suggest that an alliance had developed between

Bleddyn and the Normans of Shrewsbury. It is possible that their establishment at Hen Domen was, therefore, accepted by Bleddyn and that they advanced from this base to support the Welsh leader's campaigns in the south-west, raiding into Ceredigion and Dyfed in 1073. In response, Rhys ab Owain looked across the Irish Sea to his family's traditional source of outside support, securing the help of a Hiberno-Scandinavian fleet that attacked St Davids and Bangor, both churches being then under the control of Bleddyn. Such an attack may have been hugely damaging, but it suggests a sea raid rather than a sustained attack that could dislodge Bleddyn from the land, and in 1074 the king's Norman allies returned to help quell remaining opposition in Ceredigion. The fact that the identity of the leader of the attack, Hugh of Montgomery, is given in *Annales Cambriae* but removed from the *Brutiau* could even suggest that twelfth-century apologists for Bleddyn's dynasty sought to gloss over this connection to the Norman invaders who were to do so much damage in the decades to come.

The warring leaders of Wales had all suffered significant setbacks and sensible men may have felt that it was a propitious time for peace. Events further east may have encouraged this; in the summer of 1075 a plot was hatched between Caradog's ally Roger of Hereford, together with Ralph of East Anglia and Waltheof of Northumbria, the so-called 'revolt of the earls'. Their plan to overthrow King William seems so unlikely that some commentators have suggested that it came about simply because Roger and Ralph got drunk, but at the time the threat to the king seems to have been significant. Orderic suggests that the earls planned to supplant William and divide the realm three ways:

> to this end they fortified their castles, prepared weapons, mustered their knights, and sent messengers to all far and near whom they trusted, using prayers and promises to persuade potential supporters to help them.[40]

One destination for Roger's messengers would surely have been the court of Caradog. The Welsh leader's allegiance to Roger was clearly revealed in the aftermath of the revolt's failure,[41] but it is possible that the earlier build-up of Roger's power bloc in Wales may have encouraged the earl's wide-ranging ambitions. Roger is called 'Lord of Gwent' in a Book of Llandaff charter dated 1071x1075, where he gives his consent for the grant of an estate by a native noble, Caradog ap Rhiwallon, who was a significant power in Netherwent.[42] The estate was Llangwm Isaf, which lies 3.5 miles east of Usk, a part of Lower Gwent that was under the rule of Rhydderch ap Caradog *c.*1067. Furthermore, some of the earliest known intrusions of direct Norman rule into south Wales were around Caerleon, which was again previously associated with Rhydderch. Domesday Book evidence shows that most of the Norman incursions in south-east Wales by 1086 were between the rivers Wye and Usk and that they had made little progress beyond the banks of the latter, which would have taken them into Caradog's territory. Also, the hamlets of Lower Gwent that they ruled still tended to be under the control of Welsh reeves, suggesting continuity and the possibility that the newcomers had arrived with Caradog's support.[43] This fits with the fact that Rhydderch would be found in opposition to Caradog in 1075, but we cannot determine what instigated the hostility between the cousins, nor how long it had lasted; indeed, the two are never known to have been allies. Caradog's alliance with Roger seems to have driven Rhydderch out of south-east Wales and into an alliance with Rhys ab Owain in the south-west. In the entire course of the eleventh century, this is the only known alliance between two dynastic lines whose members seem otherwise to have been implacable enemies: the descendants of Einion ab Owain, here represented by Rhys, and the line of Rhydderch ab Iestyn.

Treachery and death in Ystrad Tywi

Earl Roger's build-up of power may have encouraged wider ambitions, which had been quelled since the fall of the house of Leofwine, in Caradog and Bleddyn. A united Wales that was part of a strong power bloc in the west of Britain may have been a dream that Bleddyn felt able to sell even to his staunchest rivals in Deheubarth, and could have been the context for his venture into the heart of Rhys ab Owain's realm in Ystrad Tywi in 1075. The locale may well have given Bleddyn pause for thought; his predecessor had nearly met his downfall there in 1047 when 'about seven score men of Gruffudd ap Llywelyn's warband were slain through the treachery of the men of Ystrad Tywi'.[44] But Bleddyn, perhaps seeing a chance to realise his ambition by following Gruffudd's example and winning the recognition of all the other native rulers as the pre-eminent king of Wales, chose to head south. It was a fatal decision:

> And then Bleddyn ap Cynfyn was slain by Rhys ab Owain through the treachery of the evil-spirited rulers and chief men of Ystrad Tywi – the man who, after Gruffudd, his brother, eminently held the whole kingdom of the Britons.[45]

The evocative word of 'treachery' occurs in all the versions of the *Brutiau*, but the account in *Annales Cambriae* is less dramatic. *AC* (B) merely describes Bleddyn's slaying at the hands of the leaders of Ystrad Tywi; *AC* (C) suggests an element of treachery by adding the Latin word *malignorum*. The *Brutiau* clearly regard the killing as an outrage that led to disaster for the country, a fact emphasised by the extended eulogy for Bleddyn that followed the report of the death of Rhys ab Owain in 1078.[46] The use of the term 'King of the Britons' is notable and worthy of consideration. It is reserved in the *Brutiau* for an elite group of Welsh leaders – Anarawd ap Rhodri Mawr, Hywel Dda, Maredudd ab Owain (d. 999), Llywelyn ap Seisyll, Gruffudd ap Llywelyn and Bleddyn – who had realised wide ambitions. *Annales Cambriae* has an even more select group, reserving the title for Anarawd, Hywel, Llywelyn and Gruffudd. In 1116, the *Brutiau* claim that Bleddyn was 'the foremost of the Britons after Gruffudd ap Llywelyn'.[47] Bleddyn is the last native Welsh ruler to be given the title 'King of the Britons', a reflection of the diminished status of those that followed him. This is, of course, just the view of one source, and of one that shows notable favour to Bleddyn and his dynasty, as the 1078 entry reveals. However, there is enough evidence to suggest that the title of 'King of the Britons' reflected the reality of his political position at the time of his death, as Kari Maund suggests:

> This claim that Bleddyn was king of all the Britons reflects on his position as successor to Gruffudd ap Llywelyn, but the title is used very rarely by our sources and only of rulers whose influence extended outside their own original lands. Bleddyn certainly ruled Powys and Gwynedd, he may have held Ceredigion and perhaps Brycheiniog. His description as King of the Britons may further suggest that he had overlordship over Rhys of Deheubarth, and in the later eleventh and early twelfth centuries, his sons and grandsons would seek repeatedly to take and rule Ceredigion and Dyfed, perhaps in emulation of Bleddyn's status . . . what is clear is that he was remembered as a king who had the necessary security to devote time to administrative reform, as well as to war, and whose reign was peaceful – perhaps the last major native Welsh ruler to rule without harassment or interference from the Norman kings and lords.[48]

Whilst the praise from the *Brutiau* needs to be treated seriously, it also has to be carefully considered. Even their favourable view of Bleddyn makes it clear that his achievements did not match those of his predecessor, Gruffudd. The latter's power was also lauded in sources from south-east Wales, but Bleddyn is never even mentioned in surviving sources from that part of the country. Bleddyn's death is not recorded in any extant sources from outside Wales; this contrasts greatly with Gruffudd, whose downfall received extensive coverage in English, Irish and French sources and even in a German one. While Orderic Vitalis referred to 'king Bleddyn' in a passage intended to praise Robert of Rhuddlan's victory over him, the Anglo-Saxon Chronicle never described Bleddyn as a king and did not even record his death. Its only mention of him comes in 1063 and the description it gives of Bleddyn's son in 1097 is telling:

> The Welshmen revolted from the king, and chose many chiefs from among themselves. One of them, who was the most honourable of them, was called Cadwgan [ap Bleddyn] – he was the son of King Gruffudd [ap Llywelyn]'s brother.[49]

Bleddyn's power was respected across the English border, as shown by the fact that he escaped punishment for his part in the Anglo-Saxon resistance to the Normans. Serious incursions into Wales from the marcher earldoms on the country's borders were held back during his reign and he may have manipulated Norman power to serve his own interests. But, stripped of his powerful Mercian alliance, his strength was insufficient to make him a major player on the wider British scene, where his death seems to have gone largely unnoticed. Such lack of regard and, ultimately, respect for members of Wales's ruling elite were to increase in the years to come.

6

The Principalities Divide

The *Brutiau* are forthright in their view that the slaying of Bleddyn involved 'treachery' and Rhys ab Owain's behaviour is consistent with his character as it is portrayed elsewhere in the same works. Although the bias in the *Brutiau* entries needs to be taken into account, the sentences that follow the notice of his demise in the entry for 1075 make it clear that Bleddyn's death caused tremendous upheaval, uncertainty and turmoil throughout Wales:

> And after him Trahaearn ap Caradog, his first cousin, ruled over the kingdom of the men of Gwynedd; and Rhys ab Owain and Rhydderch ap Caradog held Deheubarth. And then Gruffudd ap Cynan, grandson of Iago, besieged Anglesey, and the men of Gwynedd slew Cynwrig ap Rhiwallon.
>
> And then was the battle in the Camddwr between Goronwy and Llywelyn, sons of Cadwgan, and Caradog ap Gruffudd along with them, and Rhys ab Owain and Rhydderch ap Caradog. [And Goronwy and Llywelyn were defeated and Caradog] along with them.
>
> In that year was the battle of Bron-yr-erw between Gruffudd and Trahaearn.[1]

Despite the chaos, for the next six years there remained some semblance of continuity with the overlordship of Wales that had been claimed by Bleddyn in succession to Gruffudd ap Llywelyn. As Bleddyn's sons seem to have been too young to follow their father, the heir to this tradition was Bleddyn's cousin Trahaearn who, it is clear, maintained the former leader's key alliance with Caradog ap Gruffudd. Rees Davies dismissed the pair as mere 'adventurers' and other historians have been keen to denigrate Trahaearn as a 'usurper', but Kari Maund has argued convincingly that his reign was viable and effective and even, given the difficult circumstances he faced, successful.[2] However, an accumulation of blows ultimately destroyed any remaining vestige of a kingdom of Wales.

Trouble in south-east Wales

It is possible that the alliance between Rhydderch ap Caradog and Rhys ab Owain had come as a shock to Caradog ap Gruffudd and other supporters of Bleddyn. To add to Caradog's problems in the west after Bleddyn was killed, he suffered another blow in the east with the crushing of the revolt of the earls. The land of Roger and his leading supporters in Herefordshire – likely to have included men who had fought alongside Caradog in 1072 – was confiscated, the king thereafter holding the earldom directly. But some of Roger's men sought succour at the court of Caradog and, as recounted in the *Life of St Gwynllyw*, they were granted it against William's will:

> Of the indignation of King William against Caradog, the under-king. Three liege knights of Norman birth were very much decried for having formed a conspiracy against the old William, king of England, after the victory which he gained over the English at the first contest. When this was discovered, the king wished to take and imprison them, that in the taking they might either confess to having done wrong or altogether deny it. These things being determined by the king, they came to realise their execrable crime. Unwilling to wait to be taken, they came in flight to Caradog, king of the Glamorgan folk. He received them honourably, his good word being given that he would never by royal bidding do them damage, though he should lose everything which he held from the king. The king, therefore, hearing that these conspirators had on account of the crime laid to their charge fled and had gone to Caradog, the under-king, and that same man had unjustly established such a compact aforesaid against his lord, sent ambassadors commanding Caradog either to return them captive or to expel them from his possession, if he should wish to be master in his own inheritance. But Caradog, a benevolent man, fearing and shunning infamy more than the king, his lord, was unwilling to take them nor to expel them

out of his dominion, but wished to keep and respect them, as his own son. These things being related by the ambassadors to King William, he was indignant and enraged with prince Caradog. Stirred by indignation and wrath, he sent William Rufus his son, still a young man, but strenuous and warlike, with an immense expedition and armed soldiers to Glamorgan, which was devastated and burnt, losing the whole of its wealth. The army being, therefore, fatigued on its return, one night rested in tents pitched about the church of the blessed Gwynllyw. The town had been emptied of people, for they had fled to the woods for safety on account of the foe. The houses were full of diverse sources of grain, whence it could have been taken in abundance and provided as fodder for horses. Here was no provender, but rather grim famine. Not a horse got a taste of the oats. The most high God had not desired to suffer the closed house to be opened. Saint Gwynllyw prayed, whom the Deity heard. When this miracle was seen, William, still Prince, among the first offered precious gifts to God and to the church, asking mercy and pardon for the breaking of the houses. Afterwards the whole army knelt before the altar, making offering with penitence and fear, and promising not to violate the land of Saint Gwynllyw more, and never in future to do such things as they had previously done. Then in chastened mood they returned to England, magnifying the might-working intercession of Saint Gwynllyw.[3]

The long-term implications of this for Caradog seem to have been limited and he was soon to enjoy friendly relations with the new generation of Normans in Herefordshire. The Book of Llandaff records his presence as an apparently honoured guest at the consecration of the Norman church in Monmouth soon after the 1075 revolt and he was to enjoy Norman military support in the years to come.[4] But the ravaging of his lands and the loss of his old allies would certainly have been a temporary setback and would have limited his ability to respond to the challenge of Rhys ab Owain and Rhydderch ap Caradog in the west. It is possible that it was at this time that William granted Gruffudd ap Maredudd the lands that his father, Maredudd ab Owain, had held in Herefordshire, exploiting the Welsh political scene to put further pressure on Caradog.

Trahaearn ap Caradog

To try to reconstruct the political picture beyond south-east Wales after Bleddyn's death, we first need to deal with Trahaearn, whose uncertain familial connection to the slain leader has been discussed. Although the relationship with Bleddyn is unclear, the best indication we have is that Trahaearn was a trusted deputy of his 'cousin' and a leader who took over his policies, alliances and ambitions. He is associated with the region of Arwystli, situated in the heartlands of mid Wales at the head of the Severn valley.[5] The region is to the west of Newtown and to the east of Aberdyfi, near to Llanidloes and Llandinam. This places Trahaearn's power base a little way to the south of the region suggested as the heartland of Bleddyn's dynasty, close to Llansantffraid-ym-Mechain. While Arwystli may have been an early, independent kingdom in the post-Roman era, there is no way of distinguishing it from Gwynedd, Powys and Ceredigion until the time of Trahaearn. In Domesday Book it is recorded that, in 1086, the region was the subject of a dispute between Robert of Rhuddlan and Roger of Montgomery: 'Robert also claims a Hundred, Arwystli, which Earl Roger holds. The Welshmen testify that this Hundred is one of the (Hundreds) of North Wales.'[6] Such a dispute should be related to the break-up of the long-united kingdom of Gwynedd-Powys, as discussed below. The dispute was to continue throughout the history of the principality of Wales and was famously a source of conflict between Llywelyn ap Gruffudd and Gruffudd ap Gwenwynwyn in the build-up to the Edwardian conquest of 1282–3; the issue of whether the region was owned by Powys or Gwynedd was only resolved in 1536, when Arwystli became part of the new county of Montgomeryshire.

Trahaearn's right to succeed Bleddyn in north Wales was challenged by Gruffudd ap Cynan – the Dublin exile representing the northern branch of the old Merfyn Frych dynasty – who found at least an element of support in north-west Wales, in Anglesey, Arfon and Llŷn. It is tempting to speculate that Gruffudd was involved in the 1073 attack by the 'Gentiles' on St Davids and Bangor, but we have no evidence for this and it is possible that he was too young at that time. The limited information on Gruffudd's early activities given by chronicle entries can be supplemented by the *History of Gruffudd ap Cynan*, a panegyric written during the reign of his son, Owain Gwynedd. The date and authorship of this work has been the subject of much scholarly debate, but the most recent edition has established the existence of a copy of the original Latin text; previously, it was believed that the earliest extant version was a Welsh copy of the Latin. Paul Russell's edition suggests that the Latin original was written in

St Davids in the period 1137–48 at a time when Gwynedd was supporting the claims of St Davids to metropolitan status and Gruffudd
ap Cynan's sons had liberated Ceredigion from the Normans.[7] Such
a context could help to explain the attitude taken by the author to
Gruffudd's dynastic rivals. Despite the fact that they came from competing lineages there is no direct criticism of Bleddyn or Gruffudd
ap Llywelyn, whose leadership credentials were, it seems, beyond
dispute; Trahaearn and his allies, however, were fair targets for vitri-
olic diatribes. The *History of Gruffudd ap Cynan* is keen to stress the
'legitimacy' of its hero's right to rule and the consequent 'illegitimacy'
of Trahaearn's reign. During his childhood in Ireland, Gruffudd was
told that 'a foreign people were ruling over his paternal inheritance'
and it is said that 'his mother would often recount to him what kind
of man his father had been, and how great he had been, how rich his
realm, and how famous a kingdom was owed to him, and also how
cruel a tyrant now held it'.[8]

The battle for Gwynedd

While it is clear that Trahaearn succeeded to rule in Gwynedd after
Bleddyn's death, the man on the spot in Anglesey when Gruffudd ap
Cynan arrived to challenge him was Cynwrig ap Rhiwallon. As already
noted, he may have been a son of Bleddyn's brother Rhiwallon, but
he has traditionally been identified as a Powysian noble from the
well-known dynasty of Tudur Trefor; in either case, he was a 'kinsman'
of Trahaearn's. The heartland of the Tudur Trefor dynasty was in north-
east Wales, land that would have felt the impact of the recent Norman
arrival, as it included areas such as Maelor, Chirk, Whittington,
Oswestry and Nanheudwy. The Cynwrig ap Rhiwallon of this dynasty
was a cousin of Rhys Sais, who may have been related to Gruffudd
ap Llywelyn. The dynasty was to have a long history of cooperation
with the Norman earls of Shropshire in the twelfth century and with
the kings of England in the thirteenth.[9] Such a man may have been
one of Bleddyn's key deputies, perhaps someone who had taken part
in brokering the suggested alliance between his regime and the early
Norman settlers in Shropshire.

Any attempt to look more closely at events in north-west Wales in
1075 has to rely on the *History of Gruffudd ap Cynan*. Kari Maund
has stressed that this source is concerned to portray Trahaearn's

position as more desperate than it actually was,[10] but the general outline of events can be seen to correspond with evidence from the Welsh chronicle.

In Wales at that time Trahaearn son of Caradog and Cynwrig son of Rhiwallon, king of Powys, were holding power unjustly and undeservedly over the whole of Gwynedd which they had divided between themselves . . . Gruffudd [after his arrival in Abermenai from Ireland] sent out messengers to the men of the island of Anglesey and of Arfon and to the three sons of Merwydd in Llŷn, namely Asser, Meirion and Gwrgan, and to other men that they might come to meet him as quickly as they could. They set aside all delay and came and greeted him and asked why he had come. When he had explained to them, he sought more urgently from them that they might help him to regain his paternal inheritance (certainly it was right for him to rule over them) and that they should take up arms with him against those who were ruling over his territory unjustly, as if newly arrived from other parts.

When he had finished this meeting, and this secret council was dispersed, Gruffudd set off by sea again either to the castle of Rhuddlan to the noble and powerful Baron Robert, or to Hugh, Count of Chester, to beg for help against the enemies ravaging his ancestral possessions. After [Robert] had found out who he was and why he had come and what he was asking of him, he amicably promised to help him.

While he had been consulting these people, there came to Gruffudd a wise woman called Tangwystl, his kinswoman, and wife of Llywarch Olbwch, to greet him as a kinsman and to predict by a certain omen that the kingdom would be his. And so she offered as a gift to him a very fine shirt, the best she had, and which had once belonged to Gruffudd, son of Llywelyn, son of Seisill, who had once been king. Indeed Llywarch, her husband, was held in high regard in this castle and had been in charge of the treasury for Gruffudd ap Llywelyn.

From here Gruffudd finally boarded ships and returned to the port of Abermenai. From here he sent armed soldiers, namely the sons of Merwyd, to the sanctuary at Clynnog out of fear of the men of Powys and other men with [. . .] chosen whom [. . .] had chosen from Tegeingl and [. . .] into the cantred of Lleyn in order to defeat the oppressor Cynwrig. Those men keenly set out and attacked him unexpectedly when he was free from worries and expecting nothing [. . .] and killed him and a very large part of his men. At this time Gruffudd had settled in camp at Abermenai awaiting the outcome of the venture and praying for their success, when behold a young man of Arfon, called Anian, came running ahead to be the first to deliver the good news, namely that the ravager had fallen, and to claim his reward as a boon, namely a beautiful woman, called Dylad, who had previously been the concubine of King Bleddyn, just as once a young Amalechite ran to David from a battle with the Philistines in the mountains of Gilboa carrying the armband and sceptre of King Saul, and David gladly gave him and [. . .].[11]

Cynwrig's death at the hands of the men of Gwynedd on their territory is an indication of the splintering of the long-standing unity between Powys and Gwynedd, with the men of the north-west resenting the presence of 'outside' officials and favouring – at least for the time being – the exile Gruffudd and his allies from Ireland. However, the end of the union was not yet inevitable and the fact that the Latin text after the section on Llywarch Olbwch is so damaged is unfortunate, as it may offer more clues to the ever-shifting alliances; certainly in succeeding events there would be divisions between the men of Anglesey and those of mainland Gwynedd, and further splits amongst the nobles of Anglesey themselves. Some of the sensitivities involved are also suggested by the references to the rule of Gruffudd ap Llywelyn and of Bleddyn. Despite the bloody history of competition between their dynasties, Gruffudd ap Cynan was keen to be associated with the trappings of power enjoyed by Gruffudd ap Llywelyn. The reference to Bleddyn's concubine is less straightforward, but again it seems that Gruffudd ap Cynan is laying claim to be the new, rightful ruler of the land by distributing the inheritance of Bleddyn. The allusion to the Biblical story of the succession of David to Saul may be intended to suggest the need for a change of regime in the land, in order to bring about a glorious future. The author's knowledge of Biblical history is, though, rather sketchy; the phrasing of the Latin in this section suggests that Anian, the young man from Arfon, did indeed receive a reward, whereas the young Amalechite in the Biblical story met his death at the order of King David. While David mourned the death of Saul, there is no suggestion that Gruffudd experienced anything other than delight at the news of the slaying of Cynwrig.

The reference to Gruffudd's embassy to Robert of Rhuddlan is also notable. Given the intrusions that the Normans were soon to make into the heart of Gwynedd, there seems little reason for the source to mention Gruffudd's alliance with them unless it were true. This invitation to Robert may have been the trigger that started his advance across the Clwyd to the Conwy, which would see him establish a castle at Degannwy, a base that the Normans would then use to delve into the heartlands of Gwynedd. If, as has been suggested, Cynwrig and the regimes of Bleddyn and Trahaearn had established working relations with the Normans of Shropshire, Gruffudd's approach to the Normans of Chester may have been knowledgeable and calculated and a source of the future dispute between the earls of Chester and Shrewsbury over control of Arwystli.

Gruffudd next marched south towards Trahaearn's heartland of Arwystli, a move that led to the battle of Gwaed Erw ('bloody field'). The clash is not recorded by the chronicle, but it is found in the *History of Gruffudd ap Cynan* and is also referenced by Gruffudd's court poet, Meilyr Brydydd. John Edward Lloyd located the battle in a valley now called Dyffryn Glyncul, a little to the south of Tywyn,[12] but Paul Russell has made a convincing case for a location further north, just to the west of Llanelltyd and Cymer Abbey, on the border between Merioneth and Ardudwy. He suggests the small valley which runs south to join the upper end of the Mawddach estuary. The flat area near to the point where it joins the Mawddach would be an appropriate location for a battle with Trahaearn defending Merioneth from forces coming from the north.[13] Having lost 'many men' Trahaearn was forced to flee,

> right up to the boundaries of his country. After this battle the name of Gruffudd grew in fame: he was also publicly hailed as king of Gwynedd, like a champion running a race and he was surrounded by great rejoicing because he had been able to free Gwynedd which had been oppressed by cruel and pagan lords . . . he began to rule the kingdom by right.[14]

Such a statement needs proper qualification, but at this point in 1075 it is clear that the structure of the realm that Bleddyn had ruled was in serious risk of disintegration.

The battle of Camddwr

The broad outline of the events in north Wales concurs with the chronicle's timeline for what was happening further south in 1075. After the slaying of Cynwrig, Trahaearn would have had his hands full in the north and chronicle accounts say that at this point – and before the battle of Bron-yr-erw – there was 'the battle in the Camddwr between Goronwy and Llywelyn, sons of Cadwgan, and Caradog ap Gruffudd along with them, and Rhys ab Owain and Rhydderch ap Caradog. [And Goronwy and Llywelyn were defeated and Caradog] along with them.'[15] The political context of this clash is clear, Rhys and Rhydderch following up their destruction of Bleddyn with a fight against his allies. Caradog ap Gruffudd's presence at the battle cannot be considered as certain; it is recorded in the *Brutiau* but not in *Annales Cambriae*, and all three versions of the *Brutiau* seem somewhat confused about the details of the clash. Goronwy and Llywelyn were the sons of Cadwgan ap Elystan, part of a noble line from the region of Rhwng Gwy a Hafren (Radnorshire). They may have had a familial connection to Bleddyn and to Trahaearn; according to one pedigree their grandmother, Lleucu, was a daughter of Maredudd ab Owain ap Hywel Dda and, therefore, a sister of Bleddyn's mother, Angharad ferch Maredudd.[16] The location of Camddwr is uncertain; historians have traditionally placed it in Ceredigion, which would suggest that the rulers of eastern Wales waged an aggressive campaign designed to avenge the death of Bleddyn. However, Paul Remfry has made a convincing case for a battle site in eastern Maelienydd, near Llanbister.[17] Such a location would fit with the other events of the year, placing Rhys and Rhydderch very much on the front foot, campaigning deep into their rivals' terrain and threatening Trahaearn's powerbase in Arwystli from the south at the same time as Gruffudd ap Cynan was pushing down from the north.

The battle of Bron-yr-erw

Despite the *History of Gruffudd ap Cynan's* overblown references to Gruffudd's rule in Gwynedd after Gwaed Erw, it is clear that his support base was split even within north-west Wales. Following the battle, Gruffudd is said to have marched against Robert and the 'French' at Rhuddlan who 'at some time had been brought there from England and were migrating to live within the boundaries of Gwynedd.'[18] This perhaps suggests that Robert had taken more in response to Gruffudd's earlier invitation to an alliance than Gruffudd had intended to offer. While Gruffudd was attempting to deal with Robert, the sons of Merwydd and the men of Llŷn – who had been credited with urging Gruffudd to come over from Ireland – rose against him and killed fifty-two of his 'Irish cavalry and warband (L. *familia*)'. This is said to have encouraged Trahaearn, who approached the men of Powys and their leader, Gwrgenau ap Seisyll (who is described as a 'sub-king of Powys'). As with the source's earlier treatment of Cynwrig, the attempt to portray Powys as a separate realm from Gwynedd at the time is artificial and Trahaearn would have viewed the two regions as part of his overall kingdom. Late pedigree evidence suggests that Gwrgenau's great-great-grandfather may also have been Bleddyn's grandfather, making him a distant cousin of both Trahaearn and Bleddyn and – like Cynwrig – the sort of noble likely to have enjoyed an important position within their regimes.[19] After gathering soldiers, Trahaearn and Gwrgenau marched to Gwynedd 'to avenge the death of Cynwrig their kinsman' and subjugate 'the kingdom of Gruffudd'. This was the context for the battle of Bron-yr-erw, which took place in the highlands above Clynnog Fawr. Gruffudd's main support seems to have come from his Irish allies and some of the men of Anglesey, the latter said to have taken heavy casualties in the battle. Even allowing for the bias of the source material, it is clear that a significant proportion of the men of Gwynedd and Anglesey had chosen to remain part of the union with Powys, preferring this to the overlordship of the 'legitimate' line of Gwynedd and the Hiberno-Scandinavian influence that came with it.

> When the three sons of Merwydd and the men of Llŷn and Eifionydd heard [of the alliance against Gruffudd], like perjurers, treaty-breakers and helpers of the enemy they plotted the fall of their master Gruffudd and became guides for the enemy. Two brothers from Anglesey, namely Tudur and Gollwyn, likewise joined the plot even though they had received Clynnog Fawr from Gruffudd. When Gruffudd realised their treachery and that the enemy was coming, he brought with him men from that part of Anglesey facing Arfon together with as many Danes and Irish as he could against the enemy. There was a bloody and fierce battle and it was fought out very fiercely on both sides. But out of Gruffudd's army many lay killed and some were captured in battle. Ceryd, his foster-father, mac Ruaidrí, prince of the Irish and lord of Cruc Brendan (that is the lofty mountain of St Brendan the hermit, which is surrounded by nine cantrefs), and seventy nobles of Anglesey fell. Gruffudd, however, was still sitting on his horse among the tightly packed enemy and looked as if he was harvesting traitors and enemies with his death-dealing sword, just like Agamemnon, the king of Phrygia [*sic*], once used to fight. Finally when Tudur of Anglesey, the chief traitor, drew his sword and seemed to kill Gruffudd from the rear part of his saddle, Gwyncu, also a lord of Anglesey, carried him from the battle to lead him off to the ships which were in the port of Abermenai

from where they went away to the island of Adron (which is also called the island of seals); and from there they crossed to Wexford in Ireland. That unfortunate place (where they were defeated) is called to this day Bron yr Erw or Erw yr Allt.[20]

The tide turns in the south

Trahaearn's victory at Bron-yr-erw may have played a part in rallying opposition in the south to the seemingly unstoppable alliance of Rhys and Rhydderch, but a more telling blow was struck in 1076. The only entry in the *Brutiau* for that year stated: 'Rhydderch ap Caradog was slain by his first cousin Meirchion ap Rhys ap Rhydderch, through treachery.'[21] The reason for the 'treachery' – which is not mentioned in *Annales Cambriae* – is not known; perhaps Meirchion was a supporter of Caradog whom Rhydderch was trying to persuade to change sides, or perhaps he was one of Rhydderch's men who was unhappy with the alliance with Rhys ab Owain. The death of Rhydderch encouraged Rhys ab Owain's enemies and in 1078 he fought a second battle against the sons of Cadwgan, Goronwy and Llywelyn. The site of the battle of Gweunytwl has not been definitively identified, although Paul Remfry has suggested the 'bloody field' beneath Crug y Buddais, north of Felindre and close to the border with Shropshire. If such an easterly location is accepted it would indicate that Rhys was still in a very strong position in south and mid Wales and was probably in control of the traditional dynastic lands of the sons of Cadwgan. If they were trying to fight their way back into those lands it may have been with help from the Normans in Shropshire. Chronicle records of this battle are again uncertain, but Rhys was able to claim a second victory over the sons of Cadwgan. The fact that there is no mention of Trahaearn suggests that he still had his hands full in the north dealing with the threat from Gruffudd ap Cynan and his Hiberno-Scandinavian allies, as well as that from the Normans under Robert of Rhuddlan.

Trahaearn's challenges

The *History of Gruffudd ap Cynan* is our main source for the challenges Trahaearn faced in north Wales in the period 1076–81 and it claims that, after Bron-yr-erw, Gruffudd fled back to Ireland. There he was able to gather a new fleet of thirty ships 'full of Irish and Viking soldiers'; the size of an army is notoriously difficult to assess, but if we estimate a typical Viking ship of the day as being able to carry around forty men, this could have given an enormous force of over one thousand.[22] At the head of this formidable fleet, Gruffudd is said to have made for Anglesey, where

> he seized the port of Abermenai, where he found Trahaearn ruling. When Trahaearn heard of the arrival of the royal fleet, he began to be overcome by sadness, to give out deep sighs and to waste away in fear and trembling. Those who supported him in Llŷn and Ardudwy he made them move bringing their wealth with them into the cantref of Meirionydd which by their labours he had laid low, while Gruffudd transported the remaining part of his army in Llŷn and Arfon across from the opposite side to Anglesey so that they might remain secure under his protection. But the companions and his servants became angry that his promises to them had not been fulfilled and plundered most of Anglesey and attempted to return to their country with their ships laden with spoils, and they took him with them, even though he was unwilling to go. And this betrayal by his own companions was no more easy to bear for the oppressed Gruffudd than that betrayal previously by the Welsh.[23]

The unreliable nature of the source material has meant that the veracity of these events has been disputed, but the broad outline seems plausible for the period 1076–7. If Trahaearn was faced by a large, alien force enjoying control of the seas, a retreat to the mainland with all the chattels he could carry would be a sensible move. It would have denied Gruffudd's Hiberno-Scandinavian allies the plunder they may have expected, while the remaining inhabitants of Anglesey would have been unlikely to have warmed to a leader like Gruffudd, who had stationed such a vast, foreign force on their lands. The passage may also be related to the section that follows in the *History of Gruffudd ap Cynan*:

> To these misfortunes were added the following: a little afterwards, Hugh earl of Chester and other war leaders, namely Robert of Rhuddlan, Warin of Shrewsbury and Walter [Lacy] of Hereford, collected a very large army of cavalry and infantry, and accompanied also by Gwrgenau ap Seisyll, and the men of Powys, came through the mountain passes to reach Llŷn. They placed their camp in that cantref for a week, and

then plundered, routed and put to flight everything far and wide and left everywhere full of corpses to the extent that for the following eight years that region was regarded as a desert; and the populace abandoned after such a great disaster was forced by this misfortune as if scattered in a foreign land and most of them served out their harshest slavery elsewhere and scarcely any of them ever returned to their native land. That was the first disaster inflicted by the Normans and their first entry into Gwynedd after they arrived in England.[24]

Kari Maund has doubted the credibility of this passage, highlighting the fact that no other source mentions it, despite the involvement of such major figures.[25] While acknowledging that there is no supporting evidence for the campaign, it does again seem plausible in the context of the times. If the scale of Hiberno-Scandinavian interference on the side of Gruffudd is accepted, it may have been enough to alert the Normans all along the Welsh border. This would have made it easier for Trahaearn and Gwrgenau to gather their support and an attack on Gruffudd's remaining supporters in Llŷn – the area of Gwynedd which, together with Anglesey, was the most accessible to fleets from Ireland – would have made sense. The fact that the Norman presence in deepest Gwynedd was, for the time being, temporary may be attributed to the alliance they had forged with Trahaearn and his kingdom of Gwynedd-Powys.

Whether or not we accept the reliability of these passages, it is clear that the effective resistance to Gruffudd in north Wales had ended his ambitions for the time being and had kept the kingdom of Gwynedd-Powys together. Gruffudd was, however, still at loose with formidable Hiberno-Scandinavian support and this would seem to be the context for a raid he made on south-east Wales that is recorded in the *Life of St Gwynllyw*. While this event has traditionally been seen in terms of a simple raiding expedition, if it is placed in this period it could be interpreted as deliberate targeting of Trahaearn's ally, Caradog ap Gruffudd:

Gruffudd king of Gwynedd (that is Snowdonia), driven from all the borders of Britannia as the result of war, and fearing for fear the plots, which his enemies were designing to lay against him, William the old king of England then reigning, the English having been conquered and subjected because of that same conqueror, sailed to the Orkney Islands with speed to avoid his enemies who had gained his cruel success, wishing for protection and to enjoy protection. Abiding there between this plan and that, desiring to spoil and not to construct, preparing to take vengeance on account of his banishment, he incited many of the islanders towards the practice of piracy, to death-bringing gain and invasion. And so being mischievously assembled and excited, and twenty-four ships being manned from the assembled invaders, they sailed under Gruffudd's command through the Irish Sea, and after an endless and fear-fraught voyage arrived in the Severn channel which washes the banks of the Glamorgan folk. Then sailing the length of the channel, very greedily making for plunder, they dropped anchor in the estuary (or on the shore) of the river Usk. Their fleet being secured, they took their battle axes and spears. Armed they courageously encompass fields and woods. These being encompassed, they collect very much plunder. The natives who were on the lookout through watchers escape, and those not on their guard are taken to the fleet by impious hands. The iniquitous pirates, seeing that the church of saint Gwynllyw was barred, reckoning that precious articles were inside for safety and protection, broke the bar, and after breaking as violators entered. Whatever precious and useful thing was found, they took. After the sacrilegious theft they left the church of God plundered. Then they returned to their ships burdened, more weighted with crimes than heavy with burdens. The weight of wickedness was there, intolerable to all who carry it. Sweet gain and dear it seemed to the gainers, nay rather, bitter about to be most bitter to the transgressors. Having loosed anchors and hoisted sails they returned rejoicing to Barry Island.[26]

As they attempted to return to 'Orkney and Ireland', all but two of the ships are then said to have been wrecked in a violent storm engineered by St Gwynllyw. Gruffudd's own two ships were the only ones to survive because he had 'wasted not nor even willed to be participant in the robbery, nor even entered the church, but waited on the shore with his companions for the coming of the pirates'.

With Gruffudd effectively out of the picture in Gwynedd, the other potential challenge facing Trahaearn in north Wales came from the Normans. There is no evidence of hostility with regard to the Normans of Shrewsbury and it has been suggested that an alliance may have existed between them and the regimes of Bleddyn and Trahaearn, but the position of Robert of Rhuddlan is more problematic. In addition to the above passages from the *History of Gruffudd ap Cynan*, a line in Orderic Vitalis' elegy for Robert says that he 'vanquished Trahaearn'.[27] Orderic also records that, sometime after the building of the castle at Rhuddlan, Robert often fought against this unruly people [the Welsh] and slew many in battle. After driving back the native Britons in fierce combat he enlarged his territories and built a strongly fortified castle on the hill of Degannwy which is near to the sea. For fifteen years he harried the Welsh mercilessly, invaded the lands of men who when they still enjoyed their original liberty had owed nothing to the Normans, pursued them through woods and marshes and over steep mountains and found different ways of securing their submission. Some he slaughtered mercilessly on the spot like cattle; others he kept for years in fetters, or forced into a harsh and unlawful slavery. It is not right that Christians should so oppress their brothers; who have been reborn in the faith of Christ by holy baptism.[28]

This passage would seem most likely to refer to the period after Trahaearn's death, but the exact timescale of the various references cannot be determined. The statement that Robert 'vanquished Trahaearn' may refer to events after Gruffudd ap Cynan's appeal to him for help in 1075, to another unknown occasion, or may even be a more oblique reference to Robert's supplanting of the Welsh king after the latter's death. If we accept the credibility of the section in the *History of Gruffudd ap Cynan* that refers to the expedition of the Normans and Gwrgenau ap Seisyll to Llŷn, then it may be that Robert and Trahaearn had come to a working arrangement in 1076–7, something that would allow the Welsh king to turn his attention south.

Revenge for Bleddyn

In 1078 both Trahaearn and Caradog were able to focus their military efforts on the task of finally dealing with Rhys ab Owain. The likelihood that the latter was now firmly on the back foot is suggested by the fact that battle came deep in his territory, at Pwllgwdig near Fishguard. According to the *Brutiau*:

And then was the battle of Pwllgwdig. And then Trahaearn, King of Gwynedd, prevailed; and through the grace of God he avenged the blood of Bleddyn ap Cynfyn, who was the gentlest and most merciful of kings; and he would do no harm to anyone unless injury were done to him, and when injury was done, it was against his will that he would avenge the injury; he was gentle towards his kinsmen and a defender of orphans and of the weak and widows, and the strength of the learned and the honour and foundation of the churches, and the comfort of the lands, and generous towards all; and terrible in war and lovable in peace, and a defence for all. And then all Rhys's warband fell, he himself being a fugitive like a frightened stag before the hounds through the brakes and the rocks.

And at the close of that year Rhys and Hywel, his brother, were slain by Caradog ap Gruffudd. And then Sulien resigned his bishopric, and Abraham assumed it.[29]

In contrast to this overblown description, *Annales Cambriae* records the bare facts and omits any reference to Bleddyn. Trahaearn and Caradog may have felt that they were close to complete victory, but if so they failed to account for the recalcitrance of Deheubarth when it came to accepting anyone outside the traditional ruling dynasty. In 1079 all versions of the Welsh chronicle record that Rhys ap Tewdwr, a second cousin of Rhys ab Owain, 'began to rule' (what or where he ruled is left unstated). The following year, St Davids was ravaged by the 'Gentiles' after which the new bishop, Abraham, died.

The reference to Sulien in 1078 is intriguing, given the earlier suggestion that he had risen to the bishopric of St Davids with Bleddyn's backing. Perhaps he had then become close to the regime of Rhys ab Owain, something that may have been a source of embarrassment to the later compilers of the *Brutiau*, who were supporters of Bleddyn's dynasty. After Pwllgwdig, Trahaearn seems likely to have been able to take charge of St Davids and Abraham may have been his appointment. The attack of the 'Gentiles' and death of Abraham the following year is followed in two versions of the *Brutiau* by the note that 'Sulien, against his will, assumed the bishopric a second time';[30] Sulien's return to St Davids is recorded in *Annales Cambriae* and *Bren.*, but there is no suggestion there that he was reluctant to accept the office. Perhaps Rhys ap Tewdwr, having secured backing from the southern line of the Merfyn Frych dynasty's traditional source of support across the Irish Sea, had been able to reassert Deheubarth's control of St Davids in 1080 and had restored a bishop who was a proven supporter of his dynasty's ambitions.

The battle of Mynydd Carn

The epochal confrontation of this period of Welsh history occurred within a day's march of St Davids: the battle of Mynydd Carn of

1081.[31] In this battle Rhys ap Tewdwr was allied with Gruffudd ap Cynan, who had returned from Ireland with a fleet, as well as support from certain men of Anglesey. Rhys and Gruffudd appeared to be at a disadvantage as they prepared for a decisive clash with the dominant rulers in Wales, Trahaearn and Caradog. Caradog was again supported by his Norman allies, while prominent amongst Trahaearn's following was Meilir ap Rhiwallon, the son of Bleddyn's brother.[32] But after a bitter and bloody clash, the uncertain fortunes of battle favoured the underdogs, Rhys and Gruffudd emerging victorious with their enemies – Trahaearn, Caradog and Meilir – all killed. The *Brutiau* authors, perhaps conscious of conflicting loyalties, record little more than the bare facts:

> And then there was a battle on Mynydd Carn. And then Trahaearn ap Caradog and Caradog ap Gruffudd [and Meilir ap Rhiwallon] were slain [by Rhys ap Tewdwr. And Gruffudd,] grandson of Iago, and Irish along with him [came] to help him. And Gwrgenau ap Seisyll was slain through treachery by the sons of Rhys Sais. And then William the Bastard, king of the Saxons and the French and the Britons, came on pilgrimage to Menevia to offer prayers.[33]

The bitterness of the civil war is made clearer in other sources, Meilyr Brydydd glorying in the vengeance Gruffudd took on 'the kings of Powys and their Gwent tribe'.[34] The *History of Gruffudd ap Cynan* gives an even more vivid description of the bloody rivalry:

> It was a savage and fierce battle in which not even a son spared his father. The shouting of the soldiers rose to the heavens; the earth seemed to resound with the thunder of horses and infantry; violent cries were heard far and wide and the crashing of weapons was terrible to hear. So great a slaughter occurred, while the army of Gruffudd was defeating his enemies, that rivers of sweat and blood were thought to have flowed down. In the end Trahaearn was pierced through spilling his entrails, lying face down on the ground and seemed as if disarmed he were eating the grass with his living teeth. Gwcharki the Irishman had preserved his body in salt like pork being turned into bacon; in this place there fell of his household twenty-five horsemen as if accompanying him and others in the front rank; many thousands in addition were killed, and of the remainder some turned and plunged into headlong flight. Gruffudd, as was his usual habit in victory, pursued them through forests, valleys, marshes and mountains throughout the night by the light of the

moon so that out of such a great number scarcely one returned to his own country.[35]

The destruction of Gwynedd-Powys

The victorious leaders Gruffudd and Rhys fell out in the immediate aftermath of the battle, before the former set out on a vicious rampage into the territories of his fallen enemies from Arwystli and Powys:

> After [Gruffudd] had completely devastated this region [Rhys' land] with the greatest plundering and ravaging, he led his forces into the territory of Arwystli where, raging with slaughter and fire, he dragged their wives and daughters off into captivity and again avenged the wrongs done by Trahaearn with their lives. Finally, he himself went off into Powys where he employed the greatest cruelty against his enemies to the extent that he did not even spare the churches. And so with all his enemies finally routed, and their lands reduced totally to desert, he was received with honour into his paternal inheritance and began to rule, and Gruffudd enjoyed the greatest tranquillity for some time.[36]

The fact that this panegyric source seems happy to glory in the spectacle of Gruffudd engaging in slaughter, carrying women and children into slavery and 'not even sparing the churches' may be an indication of the hostility that had built up between factions from Powys and from Gwynedd during the years of war. Gruffudd's Welsh support was, however, limited to certain men from Anglesey, and his Hiberno-Scandinavian allies would have played a leading role in his rampage through Wales. That there was still hostility to Gruffudd's rule in Gwynedd is revealed by the next passage from the same source:

> While Gruffudd was enjoying the delights of his kingdom in this way, the baron Meirion Goch though bound by loyalty towards him not only brought a malicious accusation against him before Hugh, earl of Chester, but also betrayed him in the following way. He persuaded the two earls, the aforementioned Hugh and Hugh of Shrewsbury, son of Roger of Baldwin's Castle [Hen Domen], to bring cavalry and infantry with them in great numbers to the place called Y Rug in Edeirnion.[37]

Gruffudd was, perhaps, lured into the earls' trap by hopes of continuing the alliance with the Normans from which Bleddyn and Trahaearn had benefited; instead, the would-be king was seized and thrown into Chester prison and his military 'servants' had their right thumbs cut off, ending their military usefulness. This allowed Hugh of Chester's deputy Robert of Rhuddlan to advance into deepest Gwynedd, establishing castles at Caernarfon and Bangor, on Anglesey and in Meirionydd: 'He placed in them cavalry, infantry and archers and he employed such cruelty as no age had ever seen . . . the cries of the people rose to God.'[38] Meanwhile, the Normans from Shrewsbury moved into Arwystli; the events of 1081 would seem to be the key to their advance and to the construction of motte and bailey castles in the upper Severn valley. According to Rees Davies, 'From these bases the Normans were able to establish a loose, if fragile, overlordship over the surrounding Welsh districts – towards Ceri and Cedewain to the south, Arwystli in the west, and possibly Edeirnion and Nanheudwy to the north.'[39] Perhaps this advance was – as with the Normans in Gwent – rather less than a conquest. It has been suggested that an alliance between the Normans of Shrewsbury and the Welsh of the region had existed since the early 1070s and their overlordship may have been welcome in the face of the vicious assault that Gruffudd had launched on Arwystli and Powys after Mynydd Carn. Furthermore, the slaying of Gwrgenau ap Seisyll 'through treachery' by the sons of Rhys Sais indicates in-fighting between the Powysian nobles themselves after the death of Trahaearn; any force that could bring stability may have been welcomed. It is possible, however, that the rule of two different groups of Norman nobles in Gwynedd and Powys was the final blow that severed the long-standing union between the two regions. In the years to come there would be plentiful evidence of bitter rivalry between Powys and Gwynedd, a hostility that found no true resolution in the succeeding two hundred years that led up to Edward I's conquest of Wales.

In the fall-out after Mynydd Carn William the Conqueror made his only known visit to Wales, an expedition to St Davids. This may be seen as a tour de force by the king and an example of his vigilance, but the descriptions of a 'pilgrimage' in the *Brutiau* may also have some substance to them; without having taken any direct action, William already had this troublesome domain under his heel and his journey to St Davids gave him a chance to monitor developments in a land that was already, for the most part, subdued. The north was under

Norman control, while Rhys ap Tewdwr was a tolerated native leader who would be overawed by William's expedition. Norman strength in Wales was reflected in Domesday Book, which records Robert of Rhuddlan paying £40 for north Wales and Rhys the same sum for the south.

The age of the princes

After these events Wales, and any dreams a native ruler may have had of ruling Wales, would never be the same again. The big native winner of 1081 was Rhys ap Tewdwr, who was able to consolidate his rule in the south and pursue claims in mid Wales and the south-east, an ambition perhaps helped by his marriage to one of Bleddyn's nieces, Rhiwallon's daughter Gwladys, while Rhys's brother, Rhydderch, married Bleddyn's daughter, Hunydd. He was, however, to face an ever-growing threat from the Normans, who soon moved to fill the vacuum created by Caradog's death in the south-east and who were eventually to be responsible for Rhys's death in battle near Brecon in 1093.

Bleddyn, and even his successor Trahaearn, had strived to keep alive the vision of a kingdom of Wales that had been made real by their predecessor, Gruffudd ap Llywelyn, but in the eighteen years that followed Gruffudd's death the keystones of that kingdom were removed. The first and perhaps most significant setback was the nature of the submission to Harold and Edward in 1063 and the resulting inability to connect with the wider, pan-British propaganda that could legitimise claims to rule in Wales. Bleddyn and Rhiwallon went some way to reversing the full implications of this submission with their subsequent recreation of Gruffudd ap Llywelyn's alliance with Mercia, but by 1070 the power of Mercia had been broken by William the Conqueror. Bleddyn possibly and other Welsh leaders certainly made important alliances with the marcher lords on the exposed eastern borders of Wales. Some of these alliances – such as the one between Robert of Bellême and some of the sons of Bleddyn in 1102 – would be directed against the king of England, but none of them would be capable of tipping the entire political orientation of Britain towards the north and west of the country, as had happened in 1055, 1058 and 1065. The arrival of the Normans and the compilation of Domesday Book enshrined the situation as it had existed in 1066, which ensured that future kings of England would see the constitutional position of Wales in the light of the submission of 1063 and not in that of the peace treaty forced on Edward by Gruffudd in 1056. Gruffudd had engaged in a policy of aggressive border expansion to the east, but his most easterly conquests were now untenable by the Welsh and future manoeuvres would be very largely defensive.

In contrast to Gruffudd, Bleddyn was never able to impose his direct rule on south-east Wales. The importance of his alliance with his son-in-law Caradog ap Gruffudd has been stressed but Bleddyn's overlordship, if it was acknowledged at all, was purely nominal. There are also indications that Caradog's sphere of influence may have extended deep into Brycheiniog and perhaps even beyond Builth, regions where Gruffudd had maintained a formidable presence of his own. When Caradog was killed in 1081 his Norman allies moved quickly to fill the vacuum of power in the richest territories of south-east Wales; their rule there was never seriously challenged by the native Welsh and it was beyond the reach of the future principality of Wales. The Normans are also likely to have been aware of Caradog's interest in, and claims to, Brycheiniog and lands further north, territories which would be hotly contested between them and the princes of Wales in the centuries to come.

Even at the height of its power the resources of the kingdom of Wales were limited, but after 1063 – and even more so after 1075 – they were far more restricted. The loss of some of Wales's richest territories on the eastern borders impacted on the ability of Welsh leaders to maintain an effective naval presence, and this in turn further lessened their chances of imposing a wider dominion over the country. A lack of naval power seems likely to have hamstrung Bleddyn's attempts to exert overlordship in Deheubarth and encouraged interference from across the Irish Sea, an outside threat that had ceased to exist in Gruffudd's later years. While Bleddyn ruled Ceredigion for some, if not all, of his reign, his power in other parts of Deheubarth, such as Ystrad Tywi, was at best nominal and at worst non-existent. His final journey to Ystrad Tywi in 1075 suggests that he retained ambitions to rule there, but – as the later princes of Gwynedd were to find – the competing ambitions of the native nobility in the region were all but impossible to control.

It can be seen that the extent of Bleddyn's rule resembles that of the princes of Wales who were to follow him much more closely than that of the king of Wales who preceded him. Although the term 'prince' would not be adopted for a hundred years, native and external commentators were aware that a change had taken place. The decline in the status of Welsh rulers from the time of Gruffudd onwards is reflected in the way that sources outside the country were either reluctant to call Bleddyn king or failed to mention him at all. Within Wales, it has been seen that the *Brutiau* accorded Bleddyn the important title of 'King of the Britons', while stressing that he was inferior to Gruffudd. Bleddyn is the last native ruler to be accorded this title by the chronicles; it is telling that the last ruler to be so described was William the Conqueror, who is called 'King of the Britons' in both 1081 and 1087, an acknowledgement, perhaps, both of his position and of the submission that the most important remaining Welsh ruler, Rhys ap Tewdwr, had made to William after the battle of Mynydd Carn. The famous twelfth-century work of Geoffrey of Monmouth and related Arthurian literature is suggestive of the vast amount of Welsh mythology that traced the title of 'King of the Britons' back to the arrival of survivors from Troy and their conquest of the island from the giants. To have felt obliged to accord this appellation to an alien king must have been galling in the extreme.

When Rhys ap Tewdwr was killed by the Normans in 1093 and the invaders quickly overran Brycheiniog and Ceredigion, the *Brutiau* wailed that 'then fell the kingdom of the Britons', a lament that was given moving form in a famous poem by Rhigyfarch ap Sulien.[40] John of Worcester also notes that 'from that day kings ceased to rule in Wales'.[41] Although a great Welsh revolt, in which Bleddyn's son Cadwgan was the most prominent native leader, began the following year, Cadwgan was never called 'King of the Britons' by the chronicle and can in no way be described as 'King of Wales'. Despite this, the rulers of the different localities of Wales did continue to call themselves 'kings' – whether of Gwynedd, Powys, or another minor region – but the title was little more than a throwback to an earlier age, increasingly anachronistic, and even laughable, in the late eleventh and twelfth centuries. Sources outside Wales reflect this in their patronising attitude to such Welsh aspirations to kingship. The chronicler Jordan Fantosme, for example, said of a group of Henry II's knights that there was not one of them who 'did not consider himself less than a Welsh king'.[42] Before departing on the Third Crusade, Richard I accepted a pledge from the 'petty kings' of the Welsh and Scots, while Gerald of Wales told the Pope that 'Wales is a portion of the kingdom of England, and not a kingdom in itself'.[43]

The Welsh 'kings' would have been well aware of the mocking tone that was used with regard to their status, as illustrated by Gerald of Wales's account of the ribbing directed at Gruffudd – the son of Rhys ap Tewdwr and Gwladys ferch Rhiwallon – by Milo of Hereford, when Gruffudd was travelling in the earl's entourage through Brycheiniog.[44] There was a substantial native recovery in Gwynedd, Powys and Deheubarth in the mid-twelfth century, when rulers in England and the March were distracted by the civil war between Stephen and Matilda. Owain Gwynedd, the son of Gruffudd ap Cynan, had emerged as the dominant native leader in the 1160s and he led the opposition to Henry II's attempts to restore the position that had been held by the Anglo-Normans in Henry I's day. Owain's power base was in Gwynedd, he attempted – with varying degrees of success – to rule directly in Ceredigion and parts of Powys, and he contended with the Anglo-Normans for control of north-east Wales. At times he was able to claim a loose overlordship – or, perhaps, leadership – of the leaders of Deheubarth, but south-east Wales was outside his control. It was at the height of his power in the 1160s that Owain became the first man known to have called himself 'Prince of Wales', a title he claimed in his diplomatic negotiations with King Louis VII of France, and one that superseded his earlier attempts to call himself 'King of Wales'.[45] The adoption of the new title was an attempt to raise himself above the other native 'kings', using nomenclature that would be respected on the international scene. In Roman law a prince was an independent, sovereign ruler and Owain's use of the title is known to have annoyed Henry II.

The limited nature of Owain's power can, in many ways, be compared to that of Bleddyn a century earlier. The one clear area of difference that would emerge in the vision of the leaders of the principality of Gwynedd was the acknowledgement that the king of England was their direct feudal overlord, while the other native leaders of Wales were the prince's vassals. Bleddyn seems unlikely ever to have settled for such a formal acknowledgement of subservience to the English king; he challenged the 1063 settlement that was imposed on him at the earliest opportunity and seems to have sought the much more loosely defined position of sub-king within Britain that had been won by Gruffudd in 1056. But the political realities that would frame the creation of the principality of Wales had been forged in the reign of Bleddyn, and the ultimate irony for the man who would have been king is that he can be described as the country's first prince.

Figure 11 The Menai Straits

Notes

1 The Kingdoms Unite

[1] For this view of usurping rulers see, for example, the discussion of Gruffudd's early years in Roger Turvey, *Owain Gwynedd: Prince of the Welsh* (Talybont, 2013), p. 14: 'As the son of Cynan and grandson of Iago, Gruffudd had a good claim to the throne of Gwynedd but his way was blocked by the two half-brothers of Gruffudd ap Llywelyn, namely Bleddyn and Rhiwallon, sons of Cynfyn. Although Bleddyn and Rhiwallon were, like their half-brother Gruffudd, usurpers with no real claim to rule in Gwynedd other than by conquest, they were powerful enough to keep their nobility in check.' Bleddyn's successor, Trahaearn ap Caradog, is described as 'another outsider to the throne'.

[2] T. M. Charles-Edwards, *Wales and the Britons, 350–1064* (Oxford, 2013), p. 17.

[3] Charles-Edwards, *Wales and the Britons*, pp. 487–92.

[4] Charles-Edwards, *Wales and the Britons*, p. 552.

[5] Charles-Edwards, *Wales and the Britons*, pp. 555, 665–7.

[6] *The Liber Landavensis*, ed and trans W. J. Rees (Llandovery, 1840), pp. 518–9.

[7] *Brut (RBH)*, s.a. 1039. See also *Brut (Pen. 20)*, s.a. 1039; *Bren.* s.a. 1039.

[8] For further discussion of these early years, see M. Davies and S. Davies, *The Last King of Wales: Gruffudd ap Llywelyn, c.1013–63* (Stroud, 2012,) pp. 23–33.

[9] For further discussion of this battle, see Davies and Davies, *Gruffudd ap Llywelyn*, pp. 32–3.

[10] *Brut (Pen. 20)*, s.a. 1045.

[11] I would suggest that the only other ruler who may potentially have claim to such a title is Anarawd ap Rhodri Mawr, a grandson of Merfyn Frych who died c.916. A lack of evidence makes it impossible to assess the full

extent of his power, but Anarawd seems to have shared rule with his brothers and any authority he may have had in the south – and especially the south-east – is questionable.

2 Bleddyn's Rise to Power

[1] J. E. Lloyd, *A History of Wales from the Norman Invasion to the Edwardian Conquest* (London, 2004), p. 282, fn. 65.

[2] For discussion, see P. Bartrum, *A Welsh Classical Dictionary* (Aberystwyth, 1994), pp. 332–3.

[3] K. L. Maund, *Ireland, Wales and England in the Eleventh Century* (Woodbridge, 1996), p. 8.

[4] Maund, *Ireland*, p. 76.

[5] Maund, *Ireland*, p. 74.

[6] Walter Map, *De nugis curialium / Courtiers' Trifles*, ed. and trans. M. R. James, C. N. L. Brooke and R. A. B. Mynors (Oxford, 1983), pp. 189–91.

[7] The possibility that the brothers were twins should also be noted.

[8] The only known child of the couple was Owain Wan, who was killed while performing military service for Henry I at Carmarthen Castle in 1116.

[9] Map, p. 191. As Gruffudd is likely to have been very young when his father died, it is possible that the senior figure referred to in Map's story is Gruffudd's stepfather, Cynfyn.

[10] *Brut (Pen. 20)*, s.a. 1044.

[11] *Brut (Pen. 20)*, s.a. 1047.

[12] T. Wright (ed.), *The Chronicle of Pierre de Langtoft*, 1 (London, 1866–8), pp. 393–6.

[13] M. Davies and S. Davies, *The Last King of Wales: Gruffudd ap Llywelyn, c.1013–63* (Stroud, 2012), pp. 97–8.

[14] Davies and Davies, *Gruffudd ap Llywelyn*, pp. 105–8.

[15] John of Worcester, *The Chronicle of John of Worcester*, ed. R. R. Darlington and P. McGurk, trans. J. Bray and P. McGurk (Oxford, 1995), p. 593.

[16] D. Powel, *The Historie of Cambria* (London, 1584; facsimile edn, Amsterdam, 1969), p. 101.

[17] *The Life of King Edward*, ed. and trans. F. Barlow (Oxford, 1992), p. 87.

[18] Gerald of Wales, *The Description of Wales*, ed. and trans. L. Thorpe (Harmondsworth, 1978) p. 266.

[19] John of Worcester, *The Chronicle of John of Worcester*, p. 593.

[20] ASC 'D', s.a. 1063.

[21] Lloyd, *History of Wales*, pp. 12–13.

[22] Lloyd, *History of Wales*, p. 16.

[23] R. R. Davies, *The Age of Conquest: Wales 1063–1415* (Oxford, 1991), p. 24.

[24] Roger Turvey, *Owain Gwynedd: Prince of the Welsh* (Talybont, 2013), p. 14.

[25] *Brut (Pen. 20)*, s.a. 1063.

[26] *Brut (RBH)*, s.a. 1078.

[27] See David Stephenson, 'The 'Resurgence' of Powys in the late Eleventh and early Twelfth Centuries', *ANS*, 30 (2007), 182–96.

[28] See below, pp. 68–71.

[29] *The Liber Landavensis*, ed. and trans. W. J. Rees (Llandovery, 1840), pp. 535–6.

[30] ASC 'C', s.a. 1056.

[31] Map, pp. 193–5.

[32] Domesday Book, 'Cheshire', folio 263a. For discussion, see J. E. Lloyd, 'Wales and the coming of the Normans', *THSC* (1899–1900), 122–79; F. Stenton, *Anglo-Saxon England* (Oxford, 2001), p. 574; *Gruffudd ap Llywelyn*, pp. 65–8.

[33] A slightly different definition of 'waste' that is supported by Chris Lewis sees it as an Anglo-Saxon administrative device which offered landholders on a hostile border temporary remittance of tax to give them the resources to expand and consolidate. If this is the correct definition for the 'waste' land recorded on the Welsh border in Domesday Book, it can still be used to indicate the extent of the Welsh conquests under Gruffudd and the subsequent reconquest undertaken by the Anglo-Saxons and Normans.

[34] D. P. Kirby, 'Hywel Dda: Anglophile?', *WHR*, 8 (1976–7), 1–13. For the original text, see *Armes Prydein: The Prophecy of Britain*, (ed.) I. Williams, (Eng. vers.) R. Bromwich (Dublin, 1972).

[35] John of Salisbury, *Policraticus*, (ed.) C. J. Nederman (Cambridge, 1990), p. 114.

3 The New Kings

[1] R. R. Davies, *The Age of Conquest: Wales 1063–1415* (Oxford, 1991), p. 24.

[2] See M. Davies and S. Davies, *The Last King of Wales: Gruffudd ap Llywelyn, c.1013–1063* (Stroud, 2012), pp. 73–104.

[3] T. M. Charles-Edwards, *Wales and the Britons, 350–1064* (Oxford, 2013), p. 555, fn. 94.

[4] Charles-Edwards, *Wales and the Britons*, pp. 565–6.

[5] Charles-Edwards, *Wales and the Britons*, p. 561.

[6] *Domesday Book Cheshire*, ed. Philip Morgan (Chichester, 1978), 263, a.

[7] *Domesday Book Cheshire*, 269, a.

[8] For further discussion, see below, pp. 78–81.

[9] See D. Wyatt, 'Gruffudd ap Cynan and the Hiberno-Norse World', *WHR*, 19 (1999), 595–617.

[10] See D. Wyatt, *Aberlleiniog Castle, on Anglesey*, published on WalesOnline, 26 March 2012.

Notes

[11] For full discussion, see *Gruffudd ap Llywelyn*, pp. 117–20.

[12] For more on the history of this region, see P. M. Remfry, 'The native Welsh dynasties of Rhwng Gwy a Hafren, 1066–1282' (unpublished M.Phil. thesis, University of Wales Aberystwyth, 1989).

[13] See below, pp. 98–9.

[14] K. L. Maund, 'Owain ap Cadwgan: a Rebel Revisited', *Haskins Society Journal*, 13 (1999), 65–74.

[15] *The Liber Landavensis*, ed. and trans. W. J. Rees (Llandovery, 1840), p. 250.

[16] Davies and Davies, *Gruffudd ap Llywelyn*, pp. 82–3.

[17] *Liber Landavensis*, pp. 250–1. For discussion, see D. Crouch, 'The Transformation of Medieval Gwent', in R. A. Griffiths, T. Hopkins and R. Howell (eds.), *Gwent County History* II, pp. 1–45, (Cardiff, 2008).

[18] *Brut (RBH)*, s.a. 1078.

[19] For further discussion, see *Gruffudd ap Llywelyn*, pp. 74–81.

[20] While this has been extensively studied in Gwynedd, similar principles are likely to have applied elsewhere in Wales.

[21] It would also be reasonable to speculate that a high-status site in the region of Mathrafal and Meifod was utilised, although the known castle site at Mathrafal was a twelfth-century construction.

[22] Davies and Davies, *Gruffudd ap Llywelyn*, pp. 87–90.

[23] *The Life of King Edward*, ed. and trans. F. Barlow (Oxford, 1992), p. 87.

[24] For discussion, see below, pp. 95 ff.

[25] See below, pp. 99–101.

[26] See below, chapters five and six.

[27] See D. Stephenson, 'The Meifod Stone Slab: Origin and Context', *Montgomeryshire Collections*, 103 (2015), 1–8. For further discussion of known and suspected ecclesiastical centres in Powys in the time of Bleddyn, see B. Silvester and R. Hankinson, *Early Medieval Ecclesiastical and Burial Sites in Mid and North-East Wales: An Interim Report*, Clwyd-Powys Archaeological Trust report 468, (2002).

[28] I am grateful to Professor Huw Pryce for his invaluable help and guidance with regard to Bleddyn's reputation as a reformer of the Welsh law. Any mistakes in this work are, of course, my own.

[29] OV, IV, VII, p. 145.

[30] For full discussion see D. Jenkins, 'Excursus: the Lawbooks and their Relation', in T. M. Charles-Edwards, M. E. Owen and P. Russell (eds), *The Welsh King and his Court* (Cardiff, 2000), pp. 10–14.

[31] For the earlier references, see *The Law of Hywel Dda*, ed. and trans. D. Jenkins (Llandysul, 1986), p. 98, p.165. The Llyfr Colan references can be found in D. Jenkins, *Llyfr Colan* (Cardiff, 1963), pp. 12, 23; see also the notes on pp. 77–9.

[32] *Law of Hywel*, pp. 98–9.

[33] *Law of Hywel*, p. 165.

[34] Map, pp. 187–9.

[35] *Law of Hywel*, p. xxviii.

[36] Both references are in Jenkins, *Llyfr Colan*, p. 12. There are translations of the equivalent sections from the earlier Iorwerth redaction (without the reference to Bleddyn) in *Law*, pp. 202–3.

[37] Jenkins, *Llyfr Colan*, p. 23. For a translation of the equivalent section from the earlier Iorwerth redaction (without the reference to Bleddyn), see *Law of Hywel Dda*, p. 164. This ruling is related to the Llyfr Iorwerth passage mentioned above that does name Bleddyn, in *Law of Hywel*, p. 165.

[38] Translated in A. Owen (ed.), *Ancient Laws and Institutes of Wales*, II (London, 1841), pp. 198–9. A more recent edition of the Welsh text can be found in A. R. Wiliam, *Llyfr Cynog* (Aberystwyth, 1990), pp. 30–1.

[39] I am again grateful to Huw Pryce for his analysis of this reference. There is further discussion in R. C. Stacey, *The Road to Judgement: From Custom to Court in Medieval Ireland and Wales* (Philadelphia, 1994), pp. 181–2; T. M. Charles-Edwards, '*Cynghawsedd*: Counting and Pleading in Medieval Welsh law', *BBCS*, 33 (1986), 188–98.

[40] Owen, *Ancient Laws*, II, p. 678.

[41] For more on this entry, see H. Pryce, *Native Law and the Church in Medieval Wales* (Oxford, 1993), p. 228.

[42] This is particularly evident in a text known as *Rhandiroedd Powys*; for discussion, see K. L. Maund, *Ireland, Wales and England in the Eleventh Century* (Woodbridge, 1991), pp. 103–4.

[43] T. M. Charles-Edwards and N. A. Jones, '*Breintiau Gwŷr Powys*: The Liberties of the Men of Powys', pp. 191–223 (p. 194); in Charles-Edwards, Owen and Russell (eds), *The Welsh King and his Court*.

[44] See Maund, *Ireland*, pp. 75, 107.

[45] See Davies and Davies, *Gruffudd ap Llywelyn*, p. 96; Maund, *Ireland*, pp. 67–8.

[46] Kari Maund identified Cynwrig as a member of the Tudur Trefor dynasty, but Rhian Andrews believes he was the son of Rhiwallon ap Cynfyn; see her 'The Nomenclature of Kingship in Welsh Court Poetry, 1100–1300, part II: The Rulers', *Studia Celtica*, 45 (2011), 53–82; p. 54, fn. 12. For further discussion of the events of 1075 after Bleddyn's death, see below, chapter six.

[47] See below, pp. 107–8.

[48] *Vita Griffini Filii Conani: The Medieval Life of Gruffudd ap Cynan*, ed. and trans. P. Pussell (Cardiff, 2005), p. 63.

[49] His predilection seem to have been shared by his son Cadwgan, who had at least five wives/partners.

[50] For more on his accession and reign, see below, pp. 93 ff.

[51] Maund, *Ireland*, p. 82.

[52] See below, chapter 6.

4 Anglo-Saxons, Vikings and Normans

1 F. Barlow, *Edward the Confessor* (London, 1989), p. 196,
2 Barlow, *Edward*, p. 193.
3 Barlow, *Edward*, p. 210.
4 See M. Davies and S. Davies, *The Last King of Wales: Gruffudd ap Llywelyn, c.1013–1063* (Stroud, 2012), p. 105.
5 Barlow, *Edward*, p. 193.
6 M. Morris, *The Norman Conquest* (London, 2013) p. 128.
7 S. Baxter, *The Earls of Mercia: Lordship and Power in Late Anglo-Saxon England* (Oxford, 2007), p. 48.
8 *The Life of King Edward*, ed. and trans. F. Barlow (Oxford, 1992), pp. 37–8.
9 *Life of King Edward*, p. 38.
10 *ASC* 'D', s.a. 1065.
11 D. Powel, *The Historie of Cambria* (London, 1584), p. 78.
12 *Life of King Edward*, p. 50.
13 For further discussion of the Northumbrian political scene, see Barlow, *Edward*, p. 196; I. W. Walker, *Harold, the Last Anglo-Saxon King* (Stroud, 1997), pp. 117–36; C. Jones, *The Forgotten Battle of 1066: Fulford* (Stroud, 2007), pp. 110–11; Morris, *Norman Conquest*, p. 128.
14 *ASC*, s.a. 1065.
15 Barlow, *Edward*, p. 235.
16 *Life of King Edward*, p. 50.
17 Barlow, *Edward*, p. 235.
18 *Life of King Edward*, pp. 50–1.
19 *Life of King Edward*, p. 52.
20 Such an alliance could be compared to that which existed between Rhydderch ab Iestyn and the sons of Seisyll in the earlier eleventh century, rather than the enmity between Gruffudd ap Rhydderch and Gruffudd ap Llywelyn in the 1040s and 1050s.
21 The reference is found in the *Life of St Gwynllyw*, which was first written down in the late eleventh century; see *Vitae Sanctorum Britanniae et Genealogiae*, ed. and trans. A. W. Wade-Evans (Cardiff, 1944), p. 187. Gwynllŵg was a cantref to the east of the river Rhymney that incorporated modern-day Newport and the church of St Gwynllyw (now St Woolos Cathedral).
22 See *Gruffudd ap Llywelyn*, pp. 54–61.
23 *Life of King Edward*, p. 53; for discussion, see Barlow, *Edward*, pp. 237–9.
24 Baxter, *Earls of Mercia*, pp. 51–2.
25 Barlow, *Edward*, p. 243.
26 Kari Maund suggests that the same Welsh troops that had joined the 1065 rebels may have remained in the north and taken part in the dramatic events of 1066. See K. L. Maund, *The Welsh Kings: The Medieval Rulers of Wales* (Stroud, 2000), p. 71.

[27] Jones, *Forgotten Battle*, pp. 174ff.

[28] Baxter, *Earls of Mercia*, pp. 271–3.

[29] Baxter, *Earls of Mercia*, p. 285.

[30] Baxter, *Earls of Mercia*, p. 281.

[31] OV II, IV, p. 197.

[32] OV II, IV, p. 203.

[33] *The Chronicle of John of Worcester*, ed. R. R. Darlington and P. McGurk, trans. J. Bray and P. McGurk (Oxford, 1995), III, s.a. 1067.

[34] *ASC* 'D', s.a. 1067.

[35] OV II, IV, p. 195.

[36] See *Gruffudd ap Llywelyn*, p. 50.

[37] For the view of Eadric's revolt as a purely localised affair, see A. G. Williams, 'Norman Lordship in South-east Wales during the Reign of William I', *WHR*, 16 (1992–3), 445–66.

[38] See A. Williams and G. H. Martin (eds), *Domesday Book: A Complete Translation*, (London, 2003), pp. 517ff.

[39] Kari Maund says that 'the support of William the Conqueror is interesting: it may suggest a Norman attempt to unbalance Welsh politics;' K. L. Maund, *Ireland, Wales and England in the Eleventh Century* (Woodbridge, 1991), p. 40.

[40] See OV II, IV, p. 211.

[41] OV II, IV, pp. 215–7. Edwin and Morcar were not Bleddyn's uncles, but rather his brothers-in-law through the marriage of Gruffudd ap Llywelyn to their sister, Ealdgyth.

[42] OV II, IV, p. 219.

[43] Morris, *Norman Conquest*, p. 247.

[44] OV II, IV, p. 229.

[45] F. Stenton, *Anglo-Saxon England* (Oxford, 2001), p. 605; J. Gillingham, 'William the Bastard at war', in C. Harper-Bill (ed.), *Studies in Medieval History Presented to R. Allen-Brown*, (Woodbridge, 1989), pp.141–58 (p. 158).

[46] OV II, IV, pp. 219–21; pp. 235–7.

[47] B. Golding, *Conquest and Colonisation: The Normans in Britain, 1066–1100* (Basingstoke, 1994), p. 41.

[48] *Brut (RBH)*, 1069. The Welsh-language versions of the chronicle record the name of one of Gruffudd ap Llywelyn's sons as Ithel, but the earlier Latin texts of *Annales Cambriae* have Idwal. The *Brut (RBH)* version of the chronicle is the only one to state that Bleddyn held 'Gwynedd and Powys' afterwards; other versions merely state that it was then that he 'began to rule'.

[49] See *Gruffudd ap Llywelyn*, pp. 106–8. Rhys ap Rhydderch had been slain in similar circumstances at Christmas 1052 and it could be suggested that this rash of festive attacks is related to a section of the Welsh lawbooks. Provision is made therein for a king's *teulu* (military warband) and its

leader, the *penteulu*, to leave him after Christmas to enjoy a circuit of the king's townships, the only time in the year they were to be away from his side; see *The Law of Hywel*, ed. and trans. D. Jenkins (Llandysul, 1986), p.11. A possible example of this system in action can be seen in the Book of Llandaff, where a drunken *teulu* is portrayed misbehaving at Christmas in the absence of its king, Cadwgan ap Meurig; see *The Liber Landavensis*, ed. and trans. W. J. Rees (Llandovery, 1840), pp. 537–9.

50 See *www.llanfechain.org.uk/battleofmechain.html*: '[The sons of Gruffudd] were supposedly buried in the field which is now across the "turnpike road" . . . and was part of Brongain. Because of cultivation the burial mound has regrettably been levelled but is still just visible.' St Garmon's Well is now located on private land, Ty Coch farm.

51 I have chosen to favour Idwal from the earlier surviving text of *Annales Cambriae*, although it could be argued that the interest shown by the *Brutiau* in the families of Gruffudd and Bleddyn suggest that Ithel is the correct name.

52 *Life of King Edward*, p. 58.

53 Translation from T. R. Phillips, *The Roots of Strategy* (London, 1943), pp. 92–3.

5 *Opportunity and disaster*

1 S. Baxter, *The Earls of Mercia: Lordship and Power in Late Anglo-Saxon England* (Oxford, 2007), p. 16.

2 Baxter, *Earls of Mercia*, p. 297.

3 Baxter, *Earls of Mercia*, p. 294.

4 *ASC* 'E', s.a. 1071.

5 OV II, IV, p. 259. For discussion of Orderic's account of the earls, see Baxter, *Earls of Mercia*, p. 280.

6 M. Morris, *The Norman Conquest* (London, 2013), p. 247.

7 OV II, IV, p. 261.

8 Baxter, *Earls of Mercia*, p. 286.

9 For further discussion, see R. R. Davies, *The Age of Conquest: Wales 1063–1415* (Oxford, 1991), pp. 27–34 and 'Kings, Lords and Liberties in the March of Wales, 1066–1272', *TRHS*, 29 (1979), p. 44.

10 OV II, IV, p. 261.

11 OV II, IV, pp. 261–3.

12 *Domesday Book Cheshire*, ed. Philip Morgan (Chichester, 1978); 262, c, Chester.

13 R. R. Davies, *Age of Conquest*, pp. 30–1.

14 See, for example, OV IV, VII, p. 139.

15 OV IV, VII, p. 145. The description of Bleddyn as a 'great' king does not seem to be supported by the Latin text, which describes a 'handsome' or 'fine' king: *'Precipuam pulchro Blideno rege fugato. Predam cum paucis cepit in insidiis'*, OV IV, VII, p. 144.

16 J. F. A, Mason, 'Roger de Montgomery and his Sons (1067–1102)', *TRHS*, 13 (1963), 1–28; p. 3.

17 Mason, 'Roger de Montgomery'.

18 Mason, 'Roger de Montgomery, pp. 7–8.

19 OV II, IV, p. 261.

20 F. C. Suppe, *Military Institutions on the Welsh Marches: Shropshire, AD 1066–1300* (Woodbridge, 1994), p. 79.

21 For discussion of this battle, see *Gruffudd ap Llywelyn*, pp. 30–33.

22 For discussion, see P. A. Barker and J. Lawson, 'A Pre-Norman Field System at Hen Domen, Montgomery', *Medieval Archaeology*, 15 (1972 for 1971), 58–72. Thirteen of the vills were still waste in 1086, though the other nine had recovered and were worth 100 shillings. See also M. Lieberman, *The March of Wales, 1067–1300* (Cardiff, 2008), p. 40.

23 See R. Higham and P. A. Barker, *Timber Castles* (London, 1992), pp. 326ff.

24 Higham and Barker, *Timber Castles*, p. 337.

25 Suppe, *Military Institutions*, p. 82.

26 Suppe, *Military Institutions*, pp. 50–1.

27 OV II, IV, p. 261.

28 Mason, 'Roger de Montgomery', p. 8.

29 For discussion, see David Crouch, 'The Transformation of Medieval Gwent', in R. A. Griffiths, T. Hopkins and R. Howell (eds), *Gwent County History*, II, pp. 1–45, (UWP Cardiff, 2008).

30 J. E. Lloyd, 'Wales and the Coming of the Normans', *THSC* (1899–1900), 122–79; p. 147, fn. 1.

31 Crouch, 'Transformation of Medieval Gwent', p. 4; *Liber Landavensis*, pp. 250–1.

32 See, for example, C. P. Lewis, 'English and Norman government and lordship in the Welsh borders, 1039–87' (unpublished DPhil thesis, Oxford, 1985).

33 Agnes's marriage to Bernard de Neufmarché is believed to have occurred in the 1080s and their daughter, Sibyl, was born *c.*1100.

34 *Domesday Book: A Complete Translation*, eds. Ann Williams and G. H. Martin (London, 2003), p. 653.

35 See K. L. Maund, *Ireland, Wales, and England in the Eleventh Century* (Woodbridge, 1991), pp. 137–8.

36 The allegiances of Rhydderch ap Caradog are impossible to determine at this time. In 1075 he is found on the side of Rhys ab Owain, but this may have been a defection from an alliance with Caradog ap Gruffudd.

37 Although it is dangerous to read anything into events when we often only have lists in an annal, the eleventh-century bishops of St Davids had an

intriguing habit of dying soon after a change of political master. Morgenau died in the same year as Maredudd ab Owain; Morgenau II died two years after Llywelyn ap Seisyll; Erfyn died a year after Gruffudd ap Llywelyn's initial assault on Deheubarth; Joseph died shortly after the death of Gruffudd; Bleiddudd died in 1073 as Bleddyn ap Cynfyn and Rhys ab Owain battled for Deheubarth; Sulien resigned his post shortly after the slaying of Rhys ab Owain in 1078.

[38] *Brut (RBH)*, s.a. 1073.
[39] *Brut (RBH)*, s.a. 1074.
[40] OV II, IV, pp. 311–5.
[41] See below, pp. 92–3.
[42] *Liber Landavensis*, pp. 544–5.
[43] See C. P. Lewis, 'English and Norman government'.
[44] *Brut (Pen. 20)*, s.a. 1047.
[45] *Brut (RBH)*, s.a. 1075.
[46] Quoted above, p. 38.
[47] *Brut (RBH)*, s.a 1116.
[48] K. L. Maund, *The Welsh Kings: the Medieval Rulers of Wales* (Stroud, 2000), p. 73.
[49] *ASC*, s.a. 1097.

6 The principalities divide

[1] *Brut (RBH)*, s.a. 1075.
[2] See R. R. Davies, *The Age of Conquest: Wales, 1063–1415* (Oxford, 1991), p. 24; K. L. Maund, 'Trahaearn ap Caradog; Legitimate Usurper?', *WHR*, 13 (1986–7), 468–76.
[3] *Vitae Sanctorum Britanniae et Genealogiae*, ed. and trans. A. W. Wade-Evans (Cardiff, 1944), pp. 189–91. Given the theme of this book, it is interesting to see the source struggling with the appropriate nomenclature for 'King' Caradog given his obviously inferior position in comparison to William. In this one passage he is called 'king of the Glamorgan folk', 'under-king' and 'prince'. 'Prince' is also used to refer to William's son and eventual successor in England, William Rufus.
[4] *The Liber Landavensis*, ed. and trans. W. J. Rees (Llandovery, 1840), p. 549.
[5] See A. D. Carr, 'A Debatable Land: Arwystli in the Middle Ages', *Montgomeryshire Collections*, 80 (1992), 39–54.
[6] *Domesday Book Cheshire*, ed. Philip Morgan (Chichester, 1978), p. 269 b.
[7] *Vita Griffini Filii Conani: The Medieval Life of Gruffudd ap Cynan, c.1013–1063*, ed. and trans. P. Russell (Cardiff, 2005), pp. 43–7.

[8] *Gruffudd ap Cynan*, p. 59. It could be argued that the 'cruel tyrant' referred to was either Gruffudd ap Llywelyn or Bleddyn, but any criticism of these rulers is never direct. This contrasts with the treatment of Trahaearn.

[9] For further discussion see F. C. Suppe, 'Who was Rhys Sais? Some Comments on Anglo- Welsh Relations before 1066', *Haskins Society Journal*, 7 (1995), 63–73.

[10] See K. L. Maund, *The Welsh Kings: Medieval Rulers of Wales* (Stroud, 2000), p. 77.

[11] *Gruffudd ap Cynan*, pp. 61–3.

[12] J. E. Lloyd, *The History of Wales from the Norman Invasion to the Edwardian Conquest* (London, 2004), II, p. 381.

[13] *Gruffudd ap Cynan*, pp. 140–1.

[14] *Gruffudd ap Cynan*, p. 63.

[15] *Brut (RBH)*, s.a. 1075.

[16] See Maund, *Welsh Kings*, p. 77.

[17] P. M. Remfry, 'The native Welsh dynasties of Rhwng Gwy a Hafren, 1066–1282' (unpublished MPhil thesis, University of Wales, Aberystwyth, 1989), 28–9.

[18] *Gruffudd ap Cynan*, p. 63.

[19] For further discussion see Maund, *Welsh Kings*, p. 76.

[20] *Gruffudd ap Cynan*, p. 65.

[21] *Brut (RBH)*, s.a. 1076.

[22] The estimate of forty men for a typical Viking boat of the period comes from P. H. Sawyer, *The Age of the Vikings* (London, 1971).

[23] *Gruffudd ap Cynan*, p. 67.

[24] *Gruffudd ap Cynan*, p. 67.

[25] K. L. Maund, 'Trahaearn ap Caradog'.

[26] *Vitae Sanctorum*, pp. 183–5.

[27] OV IV, VII, p. 145.

[28] OV IV, VII, p. 139.

[29] *Brut (RBH)*, s.a. 1078.

[30] *Brut (RBH)*, s.a. 1080; see also *Brut (Pen. 20)*: 'Sulien was induced against his will to assume the bishopric a second time.'

[31] The exact location has not been established.

[32] *Gruffudd ap Cynan*, p. 69, records the enemies of Gruffudd and Rhys rather differently. In words put into Rhys's mouth, they are listed as: 'Caradog, son of Gruffudd, of Upper and Lower Gwent with his followers, the inhabitants of Morgannwg, together with the Normans, and King Trahaearn with the people of Arwystli.' There is no mention of Meilir or Powys and the separation of Gwent and Glamorgan seems deliberate, with Caradog not stated to be ruling Glamorgan directly.

[33] *Brut (RBH)*, s.a. 1081.

[34] J. E. Caerwyn Williams, 'Meilyr Brydydd and Gruffudd ap Cynan' in K. L. Maund (ed.), *Gruffudd ap Cynan: A Collaborative Biography* (Woodbridge, 1996), pp. 165–86 (p. 185).

[35] *Gruffudd ap Cynan*, p. 71.

[36] *Gruffudd ap Cynan*, p. 71.

[37] *Gruffudd ap Cynan*, p. 71.

[38] *Gruffudd ap Cynan*, p. 73.

[39] R. R. Davies, *Age of Conquest*, p. 30; see also A. D. Carr, 'Arwystli'.

[40] *Brut (Pen. 20)*, s.a. 1093; M. Lapidge, 'The Welsh-Latin Poetry of Sulien's Family', *Studia Celtica*, 8–9 (1973–4), 68–106.

[41] *The Chronicle of John of Worcester*, ed. R. R. Darlington and P. McGurk, trans. J. Bray and P. McGurk (Oxford, 1995), s.a. 1093.

[42] Jordan Fantosme: Chronicle of the War between the English and the Scotch in 1173 and 1174, in R. Howlett (ed. and trans.), *Chronicles of the Reigns of Stephen, Henry II and Richard I*, Vol. III (London, 1886).

[43] *The Chronicle of Richard of Devizes of the time of King Richard the First*, ed. J. T. Appleby (London, 1963); *The Autobiography of Giraldus Cambrensis*, ed. and trans. H. E. Butler (London, 1937), p. 183.

[44] Gerald of Wales, *The Journey through Wales*, ed. and trans. L. Thorpe (Harmondsworth, 1978), p. 94.

[45] See H. Pryce, 'Owain Gwynedd and Louis VII: The Franco-Welsh Diplomacy of the First Prince of Wales', *WHR*, 19 (1998), 1–28.

Bibliography

Primary Sources

A Mediaeval Prince of Wales: The Life of Gruffudd ap Cynan, ed. and trans. D. Simon Evans (Llanerch, 1990)

Ancient Laws and Institutes of Wales, ed. and trans. Aneirion Owen, 2 vols (London, 1841)

Anglo-Saxon Chronicle, ed. and trans. D. Whitelock (London, 1961)

Annala Uladh: Annals of Ulster, otherwise Annals Senait, Annals of Senat; A Chronicle of Irish Affairs from AD 431 to AD 1540, ed. and trans. W. M. Hennessy and B. MacCarthy (4 vols., Dublin, 1887–1901)

Annales Cambriae, ed. J. Williams ab Ithel (Rolls Series, London, 1860)

Annals of Clonmacnoise, being Annals of Ireland from the earliest period to AD 1408, translated into English by Connell Mageoghagan, ed. D. Murphey (Dublin, 1896)

Annals of Loch Ce: A Chronicle of Irish affairs from AD 1014 to AD 1590, ed. and trans. W. M. Hennessy (2 vols, London, 1871)

Annals of Tigernach, ed. and trans. W. Stokes in *Revue Celtique* 16 (1895–7)

Annals of Ulster (to AD 1131), Part 1, ed. S. MacAirt and G. Mac Niocaill (Dublin, 1983)

Armes Prydein o Lyfr Taliesin, ed. I Williams (Cardiff, 1955), English version R. Bromwich (Dublin, 1972)

Brenhinedd y Saeson or The Kings of the Saxons, ed. and trans. T. Jones (Cardiff, 1971)

Brut y Tywysogyon. Peniarth Ms. 20 Version, ed. T. Jones (Cardiff, 1941)

Brut y Tywysogyon or The Chronicle of the Princes. Peniarth Ms. 20 Version, ed. and trans. T. Jones (Cardiff, 1952)

Brut y Tywysogyon or the Chronicle of the Princes. Red Book of Hergest Version, ed. and trans. T. Jones (Cardiff, 1955)

Chronicle of Pierre de Langtoft, ed. T. Wright (2 vols., London, 1866–8)

Chronicum Scottorum. A Chronicle of Irish affairs from the Earliest Times to AD 1135; with a supplement containing the events from 1141 to 1150, ed. and trans. W. M. Hennessy (London, 1866)

Cyfreithiau Hywel Dda o Lawysgrif Coleg yr Iesu Rhydychen LVII, ed. M. Richards (Cardiff, 1990)

Cyfres Beirdd y Tywysogion, ed. R. G. Gruffydd, 7 vols (Cardiff, 1991–6)

Damweiniau Colau, ed. D. Jenkins (Aberystwyth, 1973)

Domesday Book 15, Gloucestershire, ed. J. S. Moore (Chichester, 1982)

Domesday Book 17, Herefordshire, ed. Frank and Caroline Thorn (Chichester, 1983)

Domesday Book 26, Cheshire, ed. P. Morgan (Chichester, 1978)

Geoffrey of Monmouth, *The History of the Kings of Britain*, ed. and trans. L. Thorpe (Harmondsworth, 1968)

Gerald of Wales, *Journey through Wales, Description of Wales*, ed. and trans. L. Thorpe (Harmondsworth, 1978)

Historia Gruffud vab Kenan, ed. D. Simon Evans (Cardiff, 1977)

'Hystoria o Uuched Beuno', ed. and trans. A. W. Wade-Evans, *Arch. Camb.*, 85 (1930), 315–41

John of Salisbury, *Historia Pontificalis*, ed. M. Chibnall (Edinburgh, 1956)

——, *The Letters of John of Salisbury, Volume One: The Early Letters (1153–61)*, ed. and trans. W. J. Millor and H. E. Butler (Edinburgh, 1955)

——, *The Letters of John of Salisbury, Volume Two: The Later Letters (1163–80)*, ed. and trans. W. J. Millor and C. N. L. Brooke (Oxford, 1979)

——, *Policraticus*, ed. C. J. Nederman (Cambridge, 1990)

John of Worcester, *The Chronicle of John of Worcester*, ed. R. R. Darlington and P. McGurk, trans. J. Bray and P. McGurk, 3 vols (Oxford, 1995–8)

Latin Redaction A of the Law of Hywel, ed. and trans. I. F. Fletcher (Aberystwyth, 1986)

Latin Texts of the Welsh Laws, The, ed. H. D. Emanuel (Cardiff, 1967)

Law of Hywel Dda, The, ed. and trans. D. Jenkins (Llandysul, 1986)

Laws of Hywel Dda, The, ed. and trans. M. Richards (Liverpool, 1954)

Liber Landavensis, ed. J. G. Evans (Oxford, 1893)

Liber Landavensis, ed. and trans. W. J. Rees (Llandovery, 1840)

Life of King Edward (who rests at Westminster, attributed to a monk of Saint Bertin), The, ed. and trans. F. Barlow (2nd edn, Oxford, 1992)

Lloyd, J. E., 'The text of manuscripts 'B' and 'C' of *Annales Cambriae* for the period 1035–93 in parallel columns', *THSC* (1899–1900), 165–79

Llyfr Blegywryd, ed. S. J. Williams and J. E. Powell (3rd edn, Cardiff, 1961)

Llyfr Colan, ed. D. Jenkins (Cardiff, 1963)

Llyfr Cynog, ed. A. R. Wiliam (Aberystwyth, 1990)

Llyfr Iorwerth, ed. A. R. Wiliam (Cardiff, 1960)

New Translated Selections from the Welsh Medieval Law Books, ed. and trans. D. Jenkins (Aberystwyth, 1973)

Orderic Vitalis, *Historia Ecclesiastica*, ed. and trans. M. Chibnall, 6 vols (Oxford, 1969–80)

Rhigyfarch, *Life of St David*, ed. and trans. J. W. James (Cardiff, 1967)

Richter, M., 'A new edition of the so-called *Vita Davidis Secundi*', *BBCS*, 22 (1967), 245–9

Rowland, J., *Early Welsh Saga Poetry* (Cambridge, 1990)

Vegetius, *De Re Militari*, ed. C. Lang (Leipzig, 1885), partial trans. in T. R. Phillips, *The Roots of Strategy* (London, 1943), trans. in full in N. P. Milner, *Vegetius: Epitomy of Military Science* (Liverpool, 1993)

Vita Ædwardi Regis, ed. and trans. F. Barlow (1962)

Vita Griffini Filii Conani: The Medieval Life of Gruffudd ap Cynan, ed. and trans. P. Russell (Cardiff, 2005)

Vitae Sanctorum Britanniae et Genealogiae, ed. and trans. A. W. Wade-Evans (Cardiff, 1944)

Walter Map, *De Nugis Curialium / Courtiers' Trifles*, ed. and trans. M. R. James, C. N. L. Brooke and R. A. B. Mynors (Oxford, 1983)

Welsh Life of St David, The, ed. D. Simon Evans (Cardiff, 1988)

William of Malmesbury, *Gesta Regum Anglorum / The History of the English Kings*, ed. and trans. R. A. B. Mynors, R. M. Thomson and M. Winterbottom (Oxford, 1998)

——, *Historia Novella*, ed. and trans. K. R. Potter (Edinburgh, 1955)

Secondary Works

Alcock, L., 'Excavations at Degannwy Castle, Caernarfonshire, 1961–6', *Archaeological Journal*, 124 (1967), 190–201

Andrews, R. M., 'The Nomenclature of Kingship in Welsh Court Poetry, 1100–1300, part II: The Rulers', *Studia Celtica*, 45 (2011), 53–82

Arnold, C. J. and J. W. Huggett, 'Pre-Norman Rectangular Earthworks in mid Wales', *Medieval Archaeology*, 39 (1995), 171–4

Arnold, C. J., J. W. Huggett and H. Pryce, 'Excavations at Mathrafal, Powys, 1989', *Montgomeryshire Collections*, 83 (1995), 59–74

Austin, D. (ed.), *Carew Castle Archaeological Report*, 1992 season: interim report (Lampeter, 1993)

Avent, R., *Castles of the Princes of Gwynedd* (Cardiff, 1983)

——, 'Castles of the Welsh princes', *Château Gaillard*, 16 (1992), 11–20

Babcock, R. S., 'Imbeciles and Normans: The *Ynfydion* of Gruffudd ap Rhys Reconsidered', *Haskins Society Journal*, 4 (1992), 1–10

——, 'Rhys ap Tewdwr, King of Deheubarth', *ANS*, 16 (1993), 21–35

Bachrach, B. S., 'Some Observations on the Military Administration of the Norman Conquest', *ANS*, 8 (1985), 1–26

——, 'The Practical Use of Vegetius' *De Re Militari* during the Middle Ages', *The Historian*, 27 (1985), 239–55

Barker, P. A. and J. Lawson, 'A Pre-Norman Field System at Hen Domen, Montgomery', *Medieval Archaeology*, 15 (1972 for 1971), 58–72.

Barlow, F., *Edward the Confessor* (London, 1989)

——, *The Godwins* (Harlow, 2002)

——, *William I and the Norman Conquest* (London, 1965)

Barrow, G. W. S., 'Wales and Scotland in the Middle Ages', *WHR*, 10 (1980–1), 302–19

Bartlett, R., *Gerald of Wales, 1146–1223* (Oxford, 1982)

——, *The Making of Europe* (London, 1993)

——, 'Technique Militaire et Pouvoir Politique, 900–1300', *Annales: Economies-Sociétés-Civilisations*, 41 (1986), 1135–59

—— and A. Mackay (eds), *Medieval Frontier Societies* (Oxford, 1989)

Bartrum, P., *A Welsh Classical Dictionary* (Aberystwyth, 1994)

Bates, D., 'Normandy and England after 1066', *EHR*, 104 (1989), 851–76

——, *Normandy before 1066* (Harlow, 1982)

——, *William the Conqueror* (London, 1989)

Baxter, S., 'The death of Burgheard son of Ælfgar and its context', in P. Fouracre and D. Ganz (eds), *Frankland. The Franks and the World of the Early Middle Ages. Essays in honour of Dame Jinty Nelson* (Manchester, 2008), pp. 266–84

——, *The Earls of Mercia: Lordship and Power in Late Anglo-Saxon England* (Oxford, 2007)

Blockley, K., 'Excavations at Forden Gaer', *Montgomeryshire Collections*, 78 (1990)

Breeze, A., 'The *Anglo-Saxon Chronicle* for 1053 and the killing of Rhys ap Rhydderch', *Transactions of the Radnorshire Society*, 71 (2001), 168–9

Bromberg, E. I., 'Wales and the Medieval Slave Trade', *Speculum*, 17 (1942), 263–9

Brooke, C. N. L., *The Church and the Welsh Border in the Central Middle Ages* (Woodbridge, 1986)

Campbell, E., 'Carew Castle', *Archaeology Wales*, 30 (1990)

—— and A. Lane, 'Llangorse: A Tenth-century Royal Crannog in Wales', *Antiquity*, 63 (1989), 675–81

——, A. Lane and M. Redknap, 'Llangorse Crannog', *Archaeology in Wales*, 30 (1990), 62–3

——, et al., 'Excavations at Longbury Bank, Dyfed, and Early Medieval Settlement in south Wales', *Medieval Archaeology*, 37 (1993), 15–77

Carr, A. D., 'A Debatable Land: Arwystli in the Middle Ages', *Montgomeryshire Collections*, 80 (1992), 39–54

Charles, B. G., *Old Norse Relations with Wales* (Cardiff, 1934)

Charles-Edwards, T. M., '*Cynghawsedd*: Counting and Pleading in Medieval Welsh Law', *BBCS*, 33 (1986), 188–98

——, *Early Irish and Welsh Kinship* (Oxford, 1993)

——, 'Reflections on Early Medieval Wales', *THSC*, 19 (2013), 7–22

——, *Wales and the Britons, 350–1064* (Oxford, 2013)

——, *The Welsh Laws* (Cardiff, 1989)

——, M. E. Owen and P. Russell, P. (eds), *The Welsh King and his Court* (Cardiff, 2000)

Coplestone-Crow, 'Robert de la Haye and the Lordship of Gwynllwg: The Norman Settlement of a Welsh *cantref*, *Gwent Local History*, 85 (1998), 3–46

Cowley, F., *Gerald of Wales and Margam Abbey*, Friends of Margam Abbey Annual Lecture (1982)

——, *The Monastic Order in South Wales, 1066–1349* (Cardiff, 1977)

Crane, P., 'Iron Age Promontory Fort to Medieval Castle? Excavations at Great Castle Head, Dale, Pembrokeshire, 1999', *Arch. Camb.*, 148 (1999), 86–145

Crouch, D., 'The Earliest Original Charter of a Welsh King', *BBCS*, 36 (1989), 125–31

——, *The Image of Aristocracy in Britain, 1000–1300* (London, 1992)

——, 'The Slow Death of Kingship in Glamorgan', *Morgannwg*, 29 (1985), 20–41

Davies, J. R., 'The archbishopric St David's and the bishops of Clas Cynidr', in J. W. Evans and J. M. Wooding (eds.), *St David of Wales: Cult, Church, and Nation* (Woodbridge, 2007), pp. 296–304

——, 'Aspects of Church Reform in Wales, *c.* 1093–*c.* 1223', *ANS*, 30 (2007), 85–99

——, *The Book of Llandaf and the Norman Church in Wales* (Woodbridge, 2003)

——, 'The Book of Llandaf: a Twelfth-century Perspective', *ANS*, 21 (1998), 31–46

——, 'Cathedrals and the Cult of Saints in Eleventh and Twelfth century Wales', in P. Dalton, C. Insley and L. J. Wilkinson (eds), *Cathedrals, Communities and Conflict in the Anglo-Norman World* (Woodbridge, 2011), pp. 99–115

——, 'Church, Property and Conflict in Wales, AD 600–1100', *WHR*, 18 (1997), 387–406

——, 'The cult of Saints in the early Welsh March: aspects of cultural transmission in a time of political conflict', in S. Duffy and S. Foran (eds), *The English Isles: Cultural Transmission and Political Conflict in Britain and Ireland, 1100-1500* (Dublin, 2013), pp. 37–55

——, 'Liber Landavensis: its Date and the Identity of its Editor', *Cambrian Medieval Celtic Studies*, 35 (1998), 1–11

——, 'Old Testament Personal Names among the Britons: their Occurrence and Significance before the Twelfth Century,' *Viator*, 43 (2012), 175–92

——, 'The saints of south Wales and the Welsh church', in A. Thacker and R. Sharpe (eds), *Local Saints and Local Churches in the Early Medieval West*, (Oxford, 2002), pp. 361–95

——, 'Wales and west Britain in the tenth and eleventh centuries', in P. Stafford (ed.), *A Companion to the Early Middle Ages: Britain and Ireland c.500–1100* (Chichester, 2009), pp. 342–357

Davies, N., *The Isles: A History* (Oxford, 2000)

Davies, R. R., *The Age of Conquest: Wales 1063–1415* (Oxford, 1991)

—— (ed.), *The British Isles 1100–1500: Comparisons, Contrasts and Connections* (Edinburgh, 1988)

——, *Domination and Conquest* (Cambridge, 1990)

——, 'Kings, Lords and Liberties in the March of Wales, 1066–1272, *TRHS*, 29 (1979), 41–61

——, 'The Peoples of Britain and Ireland, 1100–1400', *TRHS*, 4–7 (1994–7)

Davies, Sean, 'Anglo-Welsh warfare and the works of Gerald of Wales' (unpublished MA thesis, University of Wales Swansea, 1996)

——, 'The Battle of Chester and Warfare in post-Roman Britain', *History*, 95 (2010), 143–58

——, 'Native Welsh Military Institutions, *c.*633–1283', (unpublished PhD thesis, Cardiff, 2000)

——, 'The teulu *c.*633–1283', *WHR*, 21 (2003), 413–54

——, *War and Society in Medieval Wales, 633–1283* (Cardiff, 2014)

—— and T. M. Davies, *The Last King of Wales: Gruffudd ap Llywelyn, c.1013–1063* (Stroud, 2012)

Davies, Sioned, *The Four Branches of the Mabinogi* (Llandysul, 1993)

—— and N. A. Jones (eds), *The Horse in Celtic Culture: Medieval Welsh Perspectives* (Cardiff, 1997)

Davies, T. M., 'Aspects of medieval landscape change in Herefordshire, Shropshire and Gloucestershire: Evidence from the feet of fines', (unpublished PhD thesis, Newport, 2000)

——, 'The coming of the Normans', in M. Aldhouse-Green and R. Howell (eds), *Gwent County History, Vol. 1, Gwent in Prehistory and Early History* (Cardiff, 2004)

——, 'Gruffudd ap Llywelyn: An eleventh-century king', (unpublished MA thesis, Cardiff, 1994)

——, 'Gruffudd ap Llywelyn, King of Wales,' *WHR*, 21 (2002), 207–48

Davies, W., 'Braint Teilo', *BBCS*, 26 (1974–6), 123–37

——, 'The Consecration of the Bishops of Llandaff in the Tenth and Eleventh centuries', *BBCS*, 26 (1974–6), 64–6

——, 'Land and Power in Early Medieval Wales', *Past and Present*, 81 (1978), 3–23

——, '*Liber Landavensis*: Its construction and credibility', *EHR*, 88 (1973), 335–51

——, *The Llandaff Charters* (Aberystwyth, 1979)

——, *Patterns of Power in Early Wales* (Oxford, 1990)

——, *Wales in the Early Middle Ages* (Leiceeter, 1982)

—— and P. Fouracre (eds), *Property and Power in the Early Middle Ages* (Cambridge, 1995)

Davis, P., *Castles of Dyfed* (Llandysul, 1987)

——, *Castles of the Welsh Princes* (Swansea, 1988)

Davis, R. H. C., *The Normans and their Myth* (London, 1976)

DeVries, K., *The Norwegian Invasion of England in 1066* (Woodbridge, 2003)

Diverres, A., 'Can the Episode of Arthur's Hunt of Twrch Trwyth in *Culhwch ac Olwen* be an Early Twelfth-Century Allegory?', *THSC* (1992)

Douglas, D. C., *William the Conqueror* (London, 1964)

Duffy, S., 'Ostmen, Irish and Welsh in the Eleventh Century', *Peritia*, 9 (1995), 378–96

Dumville, D. M., *Celtic Britain in the Early Middle Ages* (Woodbridge, 1980)

——, *Histories and Pseudo-Histories of the Insular Middle Ages* (Aldershot, 1990)

——, 'Nennius and the *Historia Brittonum*', *Studia Celtica*, 10–11 (1975–6), 78–95

——, 'Sub-Roman Britain: History and legend', *History*, 62 (1977), 173–92

The Welsh Latin Chronicles,' K. Hughes, (review) *Studia Celtica*, 12–13 (1977–8), 461–7

Edwards, N. (ed.), *Landscape and Settlement in Medieval Wales* (Oxford, 1997)

—— and A. Lane (eds), *The Early Church in Wales and the West* (Oxford, 1992)

—— and A. Lane (eds), *Early Medieval Settlements in Wales, AD 400–1100* (Cardiff, 1988)

Ellis, T. P., *Welsh Tribal Law and Custom in the Middle Ages*, 2 vols (Oxford, 1926)

Finberg, H. P. R. (ed.), *The Agrarian History of England and Wales*, I (Cambridge, 1972)

Foster, I. Ll., and G. David (eds), *Prehistoric and Early Wales* (London, 1965)

Fox, C., *Offa's Dyke* (Oxford, 1955)

France, J., *Western Warfare in the Age of the Crusades, 1000–1300* (London, 1999)

Garnett, G., and J. Hudson (eds), *Law and Government in Medieval England and Normandy: Essays in Honour of Sir James Holt* (Cambridge, 1994)

Gillingham, J., 'The Beginnings of English Imperialism', *Journal of Historical Sociology*, 5 (1992), 392–409

——, 'Conquering the Barbarians: War and Chivalry in Twelfth-Century Britain', *Haskins Society Journal*, 4 (1992), 67–84

——, 'The Context and Purposes of Geoffrey of Monmouth's *History of the Kings of Britain*', *ANS*, 13 (1990), 99–118

——, 'The Travels of Roger of Howden and his Views of the Irish, Scots and Welsh', *ANS*, 20 (1997), 151–69

——, and J. C. Holt (eds), *War and Government in the Middle Ages: Essays in Honour of J. O. Prestwich* (Woodbridge, 1984)

Golding, B., *Conquest and Colonisation: The Normans in Britain, 1066–1100* (Basingstoke, 1994)

——, 'Gerald of Wales and the monks', *Thirteenth-Century England*, 5 (1993), 53–64

Grabowski, K., and D. M. Dumville, *Chronicles and Annals of Medieval Ireland and Wales* (Woodbridge, 1984)

Gregson, N., 'The Multiple Estate Model: Some Critical Questions', *Journal of Historical Geography*, 11 (1985), 339–51

Griffiths, M., 'Native Society on the Anglo-Norman Frontier: The Evidence of the Margam Charters', *WHR*, 14 (1988–9), 179–216

Griffiths, R. A. (ed.), *Boroughs of Medieval Wales* (Cardiff, 1978)

——, *Conquerors and Conquered in Medieval Wales* (Stroud, 1994)

Harper-Bill, C. (ed.), *Studies in History Presented to R. Allen-Brown* (Woodbridge, 1989)

Higham, R., and P. Barker, *Timber Castles* (London, 1992)

Hill, D., 'The Construction of Offa's Dyke', *Antiquaries Journal*, 65 (1985), 140–2

Hogg, A. H. A., and D. J. Cathcart King, 'Early Castles in Wales and the Marches', *Arch. Camb.*, 112 (1963), 77–124

Holden, B. W., 'The Making of the Middle March of Wales, 1066-1250', *WHR*, 20 (2000), 207–26

Holm, P., 'The Slave Trade of Dublin, Ninth–Twelfth Centuries', *Peritia*, 5 (1986), 317–45

Hooper, N., 'Anglo-Saxon Warfare on the Eve of the Norman Conquest', *ANS*, 1 (1978), 84–93

Hopkinson, C., 'The Mortimers of Wigmore, 1086–1214', *TWNFC*, 46 (1989), 177–93

Howell, R., *A History of Gwent* (Llandysul, 1988)

Hudson, B. T., 'The Destruction of Gruffudd ap Llywelyn', *WHR*, 15 (1990–1), 331–50

Hughes, K., 'The Welsh Latin Chronicles: *Annales Cambriae* and Related Texts', *PBA*, 57 (1973), 233–58

Insley, C., 'Kings, Lords, Charters and the Political Culture of Twelfth-Century Wales', ANS, 30 (2007), 133–54

James, J. W., 'Fresh Light on the Death of Gruffudd ap Llywelyn', *BBCS*, (1982), 147

Jankulak, K., and J. M. Wooding (eds), *Ireland and Wales in the Middle Ages* (Dublin, 2007)

Johnstone, N., '*Llys* and *Maerdref*: The Royal Courts of the Princes of Gwynedd', *Studia Celtica*, 34 (2000), 167–210

Jones, C., *The Forgotten Battle of 1066: Fulford* (Stroud, 2007)

Jones, E. D., 'The Locality of the Battle of Mynydd Carn, AD 1081', *Arch. Camb.*, 77 (1922), 181–97

——, N. G. Davies and R. F. Roberts, 'Five Strata Marcella Charters', *NLWJ*, 5 (1947–8), 50–4

Jones, G. R. J., 'The Distribution of Bond Settlements in North-west Wales', *WHR*, 2 (1964–5), 19–36

——, 'The Models for Organisation in *Llyfr Iorwerth* and *Llyfr Cyfnerth*', *BBCS*, 39 (1992), 95–118

——, 'Multiple Estates Perceived', *Journal of Historical Geography*, 11 (1985), 352–63

——, 'The Pattern of Settlement on the Welsh Border', *Agricultural History Review*, 8 (1960), 66–81

——, 'The Tribal System in Wales', *WHR*, 1 (1960–3), 111–32

Jones, N. A. and H. Pryce (eds), *Yr Arglwydd Rhys* (Cardiff, 1996)

Jones, R., 'The Formation of the *Cantref* and the Commote in Medieval Gwynedd', *Studia Celtica*, 32 (1998), 169–77

Jones, W. R., 'England against the Celtic Fringe: A Study in Cultural Stereotypes', *Journal of World History*, 13 (1971), 155–71

——, 'The Image of the Barbarian in Medieval Europe', *Comparative Studies in Society and History*, 13 (1971), 376–407

Jones, W. R. D., 'The Welsh Rulers of Senghennydd', *Caerphilly*, 3 (1971), 9–19

Jones-Pierce, T., *Medieval Welsh Society*, ed. J. B. Smith (Cardiff, 1972)

Kenyon, J. R., and R. Avent, (eds), *Castles in Wales and the Marches* (Cardiff, 1987)

——, 'Fluctuating Frontiers: Normano-Welsh Castle Warfare, *c.* 1075–1240', *Château Gaillard*, 17 (1996), 119–26

King, D. J. Cathcart, 'The Defence of Wales, 1067–1283: The Other Side of the Hill', *Arch. Camb.*, 126 (1977), 1–16

Kirby, D. P., 'Hywel Dda: Anglophile?', *WHR*, 8 (1976–7), 1–13

Knight, J. K., 'Welsh Fortifications of the First Millennium AD', *Château Gaillard*, 16 (1992), 277–84

Lapidge, M., 'The Welsh-Latin Poetry of Sulien's family', *Studia Celtica*, 8–9 (1973–4), 68–106

Lawson, M. K., *Cnut* (London, 1993)

Lewis, C. P., 'English and Norman government and lordship in the Welsh borders, 1039–87' (unpublished DPhil thesis, Oxford University, 1985)

——, 'The French in England before the Norman Conquest', *ANS*, 17 (1994), 123–44

——, 'The Norman Settlement of Herefordshire under William I', *ANS*, 7 (1984), 195–213

Lieberman, M., *The March of Wales, 1067–1300* (Cardiff, 2008)

Lloyd, J. E., *A History of Wales from the Norman Invasion to the Edwardian Conquest* (new edn., London, 2004)

——, 'Wales and the Coming of the Normans', *THSC* (1899–1900), 122–79

——, 'The Welsh Chronicles', *PBA*, 14 (1928), 369–91

Longley, D., 'The Excavations of Castell, Porth Trefadog: A Coastal Promontory Fort in North Wales', *Medieval Archaeology*, 35 (1991), 64–85

Loyd, L. C., *The Origins of Some Anglo-Norman Families* (Leeds, 1951)

Loyn, H. R., *The Vikings in Wales* (London, 1976)

——, 'Wales and England in the Tenth Century: The Context of the Athelstan Charters', *WHR*, 10 (1980–1), 283–301

Ludlow, N., 'The Castle and Lordship of Narberth', *Journal of the Pembrokeshire Historical Society*, 12 (2003), 5-43

Manley, J., 'The Late Saxon Settlement of Cledemutha (Rhuddlan), Clwyd', in M. L. Faull (ed.), *Studies in Late Anglo-Saxon Settlement* (Oxford, 1984)

——, 'Rhuddlan', *Current Archaeology*, 7 (1982), 304–7

Marshall, G., 'The Norman Occupation of the Lands in the Golden Valley, Ewyas and Clifford and their Motte and Bailey castles', *TWNFC* (1936–8), 141–58

Mason, E., 'Change and Continuity in Eleventh-Century Mercia: The Experience of St Wulfstan of Worcester', *ANS*, 8 (1985)

Mason, J. F. A., 'Roger de Montgomery and his Sons (1067–1102)', *TRHS*, 13 (1963), 1–28

Maund, K. L., 'Cynan ab Iago and the Killing of Gruffudd ap Llywelyn', *Cambridge Medieval Celtic Studies*, 10 (1985), 57–65

——, 'Dynastic Segmentation and Gwynedd c.950–c.1000', *Studia Celtica*, 32 (1998), 155–67

——, (ed.), *Gruffudd ap Cynan: A Collaborative Biography* (Woodbridge, 1996)

——, *Handlist of the Acts of Native Welsh Rulers, 1132–1283* (Cardiff, 1996)

——, *Ireland, Wales and England in the Eleventh Century* (Woodbridge, 1991)

——, 'Owain ap Cadwgan: a Rebel Revisited', *Haskins Society Journal*, 13 (1999), 65–74

——, 'Trahaearn ap Caradog: Legitimate Usurper?', *WHR*, 13 (1986–7), 468–76

——, 'The Welsh Alliances of Earl Ælfgar of Mercia and his Family in the Mid-Eleventh Century', *ANS*, 11 (1988), 181–90

——, *The Welsh Kings: The Medieval Rulers of Wales* (Stroud, 2000)

Mayr-Harting, H., and R. I. Moore (eds), *Studies in Medieval History Presented to R. H. C. Davis* (London, 1985)

McCann, W. J., 'The Welsh View of the Normans', *THSC* (1991), 39–67

Miles, H., 'Rhuddlan', *Current Archaeology*, 3 (1972), 245–8

Morillo, S., *Warfare Under the Anglo-Norman Kings, 1066–1135* (Woodbridge, 1994)

Morris, M., *The Norman Conquest* (London, 2013)

Musson, C. R., and C. J. Spurgeon, 'Cwrt Llechryd, Llanelwedd: An Unusual Moated Site in Central Powys', *Medieval Archaeology*, 32 (1988), 97–109

Nelson, L. H., *The Normans in South Wales, 1070–1171* (Austin, Texas, 1966)

Ó'Cróinín, D., *Early Medieval Ireland, 400–1200* (Harlow, 1995)

Owen, D. H. (ed.), *Settlement and Society in Wales* (Cardiff, 1989)

Petts, D., *The Early Medieval Church in Wales* (Stroud, 2009)

Pierce, G. O., 'The Evidence of Place-names', in T. B. Pugh (ed.), *Glamorgan County History*, III, pp.456–92

Powel, D., *The Historie of Cambria* (London, 1584, facsimile edn, Amsterdam, 1969)

Power, R., 'Magnus Barelegs' Expeditions to the West', *Scottish Historical Review*, 65 (1986), 107–32

Pryce, H., 'The Church of Trefeglwys and the End of the 'Celtic' Charter Tradition in Twelfth-Century Wales', *Cambridge Medieval Celtic Studies*, 25 (1993), 15–54

——, 'Ecclesiastical wealth in early medieval Wales', in Edwards and Lane, *Early Church*, pp. 22–32

——, 'In Search of a Medieval Society: Deheubarth in the Writings of Gerald of Wales', *WHR*, 13 (1986–7), 265–81

——, *Native Law and the Church in Medieval Wales* (Oxford, 1993)

——, 'Owain Gwynedd and Louis VII: The Franco-Welsh Diplomacy of the first Prince of Wales', *WHR*, 19 (1998), 1–28

Bibliography

Radford, C. A. R., and Hemp, W. J., 'The Cross-slabs at Llanrhaiadr-ym-Mochnant', *Arch. Camb.* 106, (1957), 109–16

Rahtz, P., 'Hereford', *Current Archaeology*, 9 (1968), 242–6

Rees, S. E., and C. Caple, *Dinefwr Castle and Dryslwyn Castle* (Cardiff, 1996)

Rees, W., *A Historical Atlas of Wales from Early to Modern Times* (Cardiff, 1951)

Remfry, P. M., 'Cadwallon ap Madog, Rex de Delvain, 1140–79, and the Re-establishment of Local Autonomy in Cynllibiwg', *Transactions of the Radnorshire Society*, 65 (1995), 11–32

——, 'The native Welsh dynasties of Rhwng Gwy a Hafren, 1066–1282' (unpublished MPhil thesis, University of Wales Aberystwyth, 1989)

Rex, P., *1066: A New History of the Norman Conquest* (Stroud, 2011)

Reynolds, S., 'Eadric Silvaticus and the English Resistance', *Bulletin of the Institute of Historical Research*, 54 (1981), 102–5

Roderick, A. J., 'Feudal Relations between the English Crown and the Welsh Princes', *History*, 37 (1952), 201–12

Rowlands, I. W., 'The Making of the March. Aspects of the Norman Settlement in Dyfed', *ANS*, 3 (1980), 142–58

——, 'William de Braose and the Lordship of Brecon', *BBCS*, 30 (1982–3), 123–33

Ryan, J., 'A study of horses in early and medieval Welsh literature, *c*.600–1300 AD' (unpublished MPhil thesis, University of Wales Cardiff, 1993)

Savory, H. N., 'Excavations at Dinas Emrys, Beddgelert, 1954–6', *Arch. Camb.*, 109 (1960), 13–78

Sawyer, P. H., *The Age of the Vikings* (2nd edn, London, 1971).

—— and Hayes, P. (eds), *The Oxford Illustrated History of the Vikings* (Oxford, 1997)

Schenfeld, E. J., 'Anglo-Saxon *Burhs* and Continental *Burgen*: Early Medieval Fortifications in Continental Perspective', *Haskins Society Journal*, 6 (1994), 49–66

Seebohm, F., *The Tribal System in Wales* (2nd edn, London, 1904)

Shoesmith, R., 'Hereford', *Current Archaeology*, 24 (1971), 256–8

Silvester, B., and Hankinson, R., *Early Medieval Ecclesiastical and Burial Sites in Mid and North-East Wales: An Interim Report*, Clwyd-Powys Archaeological Trust report 468, (2002)

Sims-Williams, P., 'Historical Need and Literary Narrative: A Caveat from Ninth-Century Wales', *WHR*, 17 (1994–5), 1–40

Smith, J. B., 'The Kingdom of Morgannwg and the Norman Conquest of Glamorgan', in *Glamorgan County History*, III, pp.1–44

——, 'The Lordship of Glamorgan', *Morgannwg*, 9 (1958), 9–38

——, 'Owain Gwynedd', *TCHS*, 32 (1971), 8–17

—— and T. B. Pugh, 'The lordship of Gower', in *Glamorgan County History*, III, pp. 205–83

Stacey, R. C., *The Road to Judgement: From Custom to Court in Medieval Ireland and Wales* (Philadelphia, 1994)

Stafford, P., *Unification and Conquest* (London, 1989)

Stenton, F., *Anglo-Saxon England* (Oxford, 2001)

Stephenson, D., *The Governance of Gwynedd* (Cardiff, 1984)

——, 'The Meifod Stone Slab: Origin and Context', *Montgomeryshire Collections*, 103 (2015), 1–8

——, 'The Politics of Powys Wenwynwyn in the Thirteenth Century', *CMCS*, 7 (1984), 39–61

——, 'Powis Castle: A Reappraisal of its Medieval Development, *Montgomeryshire Collections*, 95 (2007), 9–22

——, 'The 'Resurgence' of Powys in the Late Eleventh and Early Twelfth Centuries', *ANS*, 30 (2007), 182–96

——, 'The Whole Land between Dyfi and Dulas', *Montgomeryshire Collections*, 95 (2007), 1–8

Strange, W. A., 'The Rise and Fall of a Saint's Community: Llandeilo Fawr, 600–1200', *Journal of Welsh Religious History*, 2 (2002), 1–18

Strickland, M. (ed.), *Anglo-Norman Warfare* (Woodbridge, 1992)

——, 'Military Technology and Conquest: The Anomaly of Anglo-Saxon England', *ANS*, 19 (1996), 353–82

——, *War and Chivalry: The Conduct and Perception of War in England and Normandy, 1066–1217* (Cambridge, 1996)

Suppe, F.C., 'The cultural significance of decapitation in high medieval Wales and the Marches', *BBCS*, 36 (1989), 147–60

——, 'Interpreter Families and Anglo-Welsh relations in the Shropshire-Powys Marches in the Twelfth Century', *ANS*, 30 (2007), 196–212

——, *Military Institutions on the Welsh Marches: Shropshire, AD 1066–1300* (Woodbridge, 1994)

——, 'Roger of Powys, Henry II's Anglo-Welsh Middleman, and his Lineage', *WHR*, 21 (2002), 1–23

——, 'Who was Rhys Sais? Some Comments on Anglo-Welsh relations before 1066', *Haskins Society Journal*, 7 (1995), 63–73

Thornton, D. E., 'Maredudd ab Owain (d. 999): The Most Famous King of the Welsh', *WHR*, 18 (1997), 567–91

——, 'Who was Rhain the Irishman?', *Studia Celtica*, 34 (2000), 131–48

Turvey, R., 'The Death and Burial of an Excommunicate Prince: The Lord Rhys and the Cathedral Church of St Davids', *Journal Pembs. Hist. Soc.*, 7 (1996–7), 26–49

——, 'The Defences of Twelfth-Century Deheubarth and the Castle Strategy of the Lord Rhys', *Arch. Camb.*, 144 (1995), 103–32

——, *The Lord Rhys, Prince of Deheubarth* (Llandysul, 1997)

Owain Gwynedd: Prince of the Welsh (Talybont, 2013)

Van Houts, A. E., 'The Norman Conquest through European Eyes', *EHR*, 110 (1995), 832–53

Wainwright, F. T., 'Cledemutha', *EHR*, 65 (1950), 203–12

Walker, D., 'A Note on Gruffudd ap Llywelyn', *WHR*, 1 (1960–3), 83–94

——, 'William fitz Osbern and the Norman Settlement in Herefordshire', *TWNFC*, 39 (1967–9), 402–12

Walker, I. W., *Harold, the Last Anglo-Saxon King* (Stroud, 1997)

——, *Mercia and the Origins of England* (Stroud, 2000)

Warrington, W., *The History of Wales* (4th edn., Brecon, 1823)

Whitelock, D., et al. (eds.), *The Norman Conquest* (London, 1966)

Wilkinson, P. F., 'Excavations at Hen Gastell, Briton Ferry, West Glamorgan, 1991–2', *Medieval Archaeology*, 39 (1995), 1–50

Williams, A. G., 'Norman Lordship in South-east Wales during the Reign of William I', *WHR*, 16 (1992–3), 445–66

——, 'The Norman lordship of Glamorgan: An examination of its establishment and development' (unpublished MPhil thesis, University of Wales Cardiff, 1991)

Wyatt, D., 'Gruffudd ap Cynan and the Hiberno-Norse World,' *WHR*, 19 (1999), 595–617

Index